Leviticus
for You and Me

John Iles

Self-published by   John Iles, Royston, Hertfordshire, United Kingdom
                      johnarthur1939@icloud.com

First published 2016

British Library Cataloguing in Publication Data
A catalogue record for this book is available from the British Library.

ISBN: 978-1-5272-0029-1

Contents

Introduction

It may seem like stating the obvious to begin by saying that the book of Leviticus contains instructions for God's people. But it is important to bear in mind when reading Leviticus that God had already established the Hebrews as His people before He gave these instructions to Moses. The purpose of the book is not to explain how they could become God's people, but how that relationship was to be maintained.

The slaves of Egypt became the people of God in three stages, each of which demonstrates a requirement for becoming God's people. Those three requirements are God's sacrifice, God's covenant and God's presence.

God's sacrifice

In one of the best known stories of the Bible, God sent ten plagues to force Pharaoh to release the Hebrew slaves. The final plague was that every first-born in Egypt would die. Every Israelite family was to kill a perfect lamb and apply its blood to the doorframe of their house. God said, "When I see the blood, I will pass over you." (Exodus 12) Those who sheltered beneath the blood were protected and their first-born lived.

God's covenant

Moses led the people to Sinai where God said that if they would keep His covenant by obeying Him they would be His own, special people (Exodus 19:5). The Ten Commandments summarise what God required. The people's response was that they would obey (Exodus 24:7).

God's presence

On Mount Sinai, God told Moses to build a special tent, the Tabernacle, in which God could dwell among His people (Exodus 25:8). Moses built the Tabernacle exactly as God had shown him. When it was complete "the glory of the LORD filled the tabernacle" (Exodus 40:34). God had come to dwell among His people. It was from that tent that God spoke to Moses the words recorded in Leviticus (Leviticus 1:1).

The same three requirements remain today for those who would be God's people.

God's Final Sacrifice

When Jesus wanted to explain the significance of His death and to give His disciples something to remember Him by, He used the Passover - "this is my body ... this is my blood".

1

He returned to Jerusalem at such a time and entered the city in such a manner that, in spite of the Jewish leaders' plans that it would not happen during the feast, (Matthew 26:5) He ensured that He would in fact die at Passover time.

Through the Passover the Israelites were rescued from slavery to serve God. In the same way, God, through the sacrifice of Jesus, "has delivered us from the domain of darkness and transferred us to the kingdom of His beloved Son." (Colossians 1:13-14)

God's New Covenant

In spite of good intentions, the Israelites failed to keep the covenant. So God promised to make a new covenant under which He would write His law on their hearts and "I will be their God and they shall be my people" and "I will forgive their iniquity, and I will remember their sin no more." (Jeremiah 31:31-34)

The Lord Jesus, at the Last Supper, as He passed round the cup of wine said, "This cup that is poured out for you is the new covenant in my blood." (Luke 22:20) This covenant will never fail because it depends, not on our law-keeping, but entirely on God's grace. Those who trust in Christ's sacrifice are God's forever, sealed with and by the Holy Spirit. (Ephesians 4:1, 30)

God's Eternal Presence

Jesus, having died, risen and ascended into heaven, poured out the Holy Spirit upon and into the Church. (Acts 2:33) Believers of whatever nationality "are being built together into a dwelling place for God by the Spirit." (Ephesians 2:22) Every individual who is a true believer in Christ is indwelt by the Spirit of God. (Romans 8.9; 1 Corinthians 6:19)

Just as God's dealings with the Israelites have their fulfilment in Christ, so do the sacrifices, rituals and rules of the book of Leviticus.

The Burnt Offering
Exodus 40:34 to Leviticus 1:17

I wonder what thoughts were going through people's minds as Moses went up Sinai (Exodus 19). God had called Moses to go up but the people were barred from even touching the mountain.

Perhaps there were those who were indignant that Moses was allowed to go up to meet God but they were not. At a later date, Aaron and Miriam reacted like that when Moses had done something of which they evidently did not approve and they protested, "Has the LORD indeed spoken only through Moses? Has he not spoken through us also?" (Numbers 12:2)

On the day that Moses went up into the mountain "there were thunders and lightnings and a thick cloud on the mountain and a very loud trumpet blast, so that all the people in the camp trembled". So there may have been those who had no desire to go anywhere near Sinai. Perhaps some felt they could not get far enough away.

As, sometime later, they saw the Tabernacle taking shape, the same range of emotions may have been present; it was even possible that some were quite indifferent to what was going on.

God Unapproachable?

However, if any thought that now they would be free to enter God's presence at will they were wrong. When the erection of the Tabernacle was complete, God descended in cloud and fire and His glory filled the Tabernacle so that even Moses was unable to enter. And this was not a temporary situation. In Exodus 40:38 we are told "the cloud of the LORD was on the Tabernacle by day, and fire was in it by night, in the sight of all the house of Israel throughout all their journeys".

This demonstrates what the God/Man relationship is like. Isaiah clearly states the problem: "Your iniquities have made a separation between you and your God, and your sins have hidden his face from you" (Isaiah 59:2). There is no right of access into the presence of God unless the problem of our breaking God's laws is dealt with.

So those who thought that with the Tabernacle being right in the middle of the camp they would be able to enter God's presence whenever and however they liked were wrong.

3

God's Intention

On the other hand, those who thought of keeping their distance or were totally indifferent were also wrong, because it is God's intention to have fellowship with those who are His people.

That has been God's intention from the beginning. In Genesis 2 and 3 it is written that God made a garden for Man. He brought the animals to Man for him to name. And God would, evidently, walk "in the garden in the cool of the day" (Genesis 3:8).

God's intention is shown in the giving of the Law on Sinai. It was God who took the initiative: "the LORD called Moses to the top of the mountain, and Moses went up" (Exodus 19:20).

It is shown in the fact that the Law was not only about morals and justice, and how to live together as a society, but it was also about making arrangements for God to live among them: "let them make me a sanctuary, that I may dwell in their midst" (Exodus 25:8). And the details for the construction of that sanctuary did not come from Moses, but God showed him the pattern to follow (Exodus 25:9).

God's intention to have fellowship with His people is shown in Exodus 40. Moses did not have to plead with God to come among them. When Moses had finished the work as God had instructed him, "Then the cloud covered the tent of meeting, and the glory of the LORD filled the tabernacle" (Exodus 40:33-34). This was God's choice. The whole purpose of the Tabernacle was so that God would dwell among them (Exodus 25:8).

It is God's desire and intention to have fellowship with His people. In fact, the distinguishing mark of the people of God was and is to be, not only lives lived according to certain rules, but God's presence among them. The two go inseparably together.

God's Initiative in Leviticus

In the first verse of Leviticus we are told that, out of the cloud, the fire and the glory, "The LORD called Moses and spoke to him". In fact, twenty-eight times in Leviticus we read, "The LORD spoke to Moses". Throughout the giving of the ceremonial laws it is God who takes the initiative as God explains the way in which His people should approach Him.

In the first few verses of this book other details show that what God has in mind is fellowship with His people. For instance the tabernacle is described as

4

"the tent of *meeting*" (Leviticus 1:1); the word translated "offering" in verse 2 has the root idea of "coming near"; three times in this first chapter (3, 5 and 11) the phrase "before the LORD" is used.

God wants fellowship with His people; He wants them to be in harmony with Him.

God's Way of Approach

Throughout the chapter the instructions as to what is to be offered and the way it is to be dealt with are given as commands: "you shall", "he shall", "the priest shall". The one who would approach God must do so in God's way.

It is not that the way of approach is made difficult. "Any one of you" (verse 2) God says may come. Poverty is not a barrier since a bull, a sheep or goat, a dove or a pigeon are acceptable.

It is not that just anything would be accepted. This was not an opportunity to be rid of unwanted, unproductive, diseased, injured or deformed animals or birds. What was offered had to be "without blemish" (3 and 10) so that some cost was involved, however small.

There is no indication that God demanded a more costly sacrifice from those who were more prosperous. The worshipper would give what he could afford and his generosity would be determined by the gratitude of his heart. And attitude of heart has always been most important to God. As David wrote, "You will not delight in sacrifice, or I would give it; you will not be pleased with a burnt offering. The sacrifices of God are a broken spirit; a broken and contrite heart, O God, you will not despise" (Psalm 51:16-17).

God invites His people to meet with Him; but they must come in His way.

God's Explanation

God explained why He specified this means of approach. He told Moses that the burnt offering "shall be accepted for [the worshipper] to make atonement for him" (4). Atonement, "at-one-ment" would be made. Worshipper and God would be at one, in harmony. The burnt offering achieves this because it is a blood offering. As God explains in 17.11, "The life of the flesh is in the blood, and I have given it for you on the altar to make atonement for your souls, for it is the blood that makes atonement by the life."

Bloodless offerings are detailed in this book. The grain offering (Leviticus 2) and the first-fruits of harvest (Leviticus 23) are bloodless offerings, acknowledgements of God's provision and a way of giving thanks. But an approach to God must be on the basis of the shedding of blood.

God warned Adam that if he were to disobey God by eating of the tree of the knowledge of good and evil he would die. Paul reminds the Christians in Rome of this in the famous statement that "the wages of sin is death" (Romans 6:23). So for the sinner to live, atonement must be made. A life must be given in order to save the life of the worshipper.

The instructions here are, "He shall lay his hand on the head of the burnt offering, and it shall be accepted for him to make atonement for him" (4). The worshipper identifies with the animal by laying his hand on its head and it is "accepted for him", the animal dies in his place and atonement is made.

Some offerings in Leviticus are prescribed in order to deal with specific sins. But this is not the case with the burnt offering. Not one of the Hebrew words for sin is used in this chapter. The problem is not simply what we do but what we are. We have a sinful nature, and it is what we *are* that separates us from a God who is totally separate from sin. The purpose of the burnt offering is not "that he may be forgiven" but "that he may be *accepted* before the LORD" (3). The burnt offering was to deal with the worshipper's sinful nature.

The Burnt Offering Speaks of Jesus

Perhaps this goes without saying but it can be a helpful reminder. God took the initiative for the Hebrews and, in His Son, God took the initiative for us all: "the Father has sent his Son to be the Saviour of the world" (1 John 4.14). The Hebrews had to come in God's way, and so do we. Jesus said, "I am the way, and the truth, and the life. No one comes to the Father except through me" (John 14:6).

Jesus made the way by the sacrifice of Himself: "Christ loved us and gave himself up *for us* [in our place], a fragrant offering and sacrifice to God" (Ephesians 5:2). That offering was accepted because Christ "offered himself *without blemish* to God" (Hebrews 9:14).

The Hebrew worshipper had to identify with the offering. The worshipper had to bring it to the entrance of the tabernacle (3); he had to lay his hand on the animal's head (4); he had to kill it in God's presence (5); and he had to skin and cut it into pieces (6). So he was actively and personally involved in everything except pouring out the blood and arranging the pieces on the altar. Those two things the priest did. So, as far as possible, the worshipper

6

identified with the sacrifice of the animal. He was acknowledging that he deserved to be excluded and was offering the animal as a substitute. This was what God had asked for and so "it shall be **accepted for him** to make atonement for him" (4).

Maybe the most telling of everything that the worshipper had to do was the laying of the hand on the head of the animal.

In the churches to which I was taken as a child, a hymn by Isaac Watts was often sung in the communion services:

> Not all the blood of beasts
> On Jewish altars slain
> Could give the guilty conscience peace
> Or wash away the stain.

> But Christ, the heavenly Lamb,
> Takes all our sins away;
> A sacrifice of nobler name
> And richer blood than they.

> My faith would lay her hand
> On that dear head of Thine,
> While, like a penitent, I stand,
> And there confess my sin.

The Burnt Offering and the Christian Life

The burnt offering was a sacrifice for those who were God's people. So it teaches us, not only about becoming God's people, but also about being God's people. It illustrates what Christ's death means for me now that, through Christ, I am a child of God.

Firstly, it is a reminder that there can only ever be one means of approach to God.

The apostle Paul wrote, "Therefore, since we have been justified by faith, we have peace with God through our Lord Jesus Christ. Through him we have also obtained access by faith into this grace in which we stand" (Romans 5:1-2). We have been justified, we have peace with God and, as a result, we have access. That is we have someone to introduce us into the presence of the

7

King. All this is possible only "through our Lord Jesus Christ". We and what we offer, our service, our prayers are accepted only because of Jesus. I never will be able to approach God on any other basis.

Secondly, the burnt offering illustrates the fact that there is one sacrifice to imitate.

The worshipper identifies as completely as possible with the victim: bringing it to the entrance; the laying of the hand on its head; the killing; the skinning; the butchering. Then it is completely burnt on the altar - "the priest shall burn **all of it** on the altar" (9). In symbol the worshipper is dedicating himself completely to God and His ways. This is emphasised by the description of the sacrifice as "a food offering with *a pleasing aroma* to the LORD" (9). In symbol, the worshipper was dedicating himself to a life pleasing to God.

Paul reminds the Christians at Ephesus that "Christ loved us and gave himself up for us, a fragrant offering and sacrifice to God" (Ephesians 5:2). And Jesus calls us to follow Him. He said, "This is my commandment, that you love one another as I have loved you. Greater love has no one than this, that someone lay down his life for his friends" (John 15:12-13).

Finally, the burnt offering shows that living to please God is costly.

Whatever animal or bird was offered, it cost the worshipper something. King David said, "I will not offer burnt offerings to the LORD my God that cost me nothing" (2 Samuel 24:24).

Paul reminds the Galatians that there are two things that should motivate them to "live by the Spirit". One is that they belong to Christ Jesus and the second is that when they gave themselves to Christ they "crucified the flesh with its passions and desires" (Galatians 5:24). These two things define what it means to be a Christian, to live as a Christian, and they pervade the New Testament teaching about living the Christian life. "You are not your own, for you were bought with a price. So glorify God in your body." (1 Corinthians 6:19-20)

Although Christ paid the price and salvation is free, yet to follow Him costs everything since in order to do so we must deny ourselves and "take up the cross" every day (Luke 9:23).

The Grain Offering
Leviticus 2

As Christmas approaches the perennial question arises for my wife and me, "What do we buy as presents for those who seem to have everything?" Usually, for our children and grandchildren, we have gone for the easy option and given money. While this chapter was in preparation the question arose and we had taken the money route for two of our families when our daughter had a great idea. So our third family got a hamper. What a success! They'll probably all get hampers in future! Problem solved and we only have to think about it once a year.

A Gift for God

But the question that ought to be occupying my thinking every moment of every day is, "What should I give to God?" He doesn't need anything; what can He possibly want from me?

This chapter of Leviticus answers that question.

The word translated "food" (NKJV), "cereal" (RSV), "grain" (ESV; NIV) is the Hebrew word for "gift". It is used in Leviticus only here. No other offering is described as a gift. But the word is used in various ways in the Old Testament, and each way illustrates some aspect of what giving to God means.

When Joseph's brothers went to Egypt for the second time, "they brought into the house to him the present that they had with them and bowed down to him to the ground" (Genesis 43:26). So giving a gift may be an acknowledgement of the fact that one is in the presence of a superior.

When Saul was appointed king (1 Samuel 10:27) some refused to bring a present to Saul as a deliberate show of disrespect. The inference is that those who did accept Saul as king did bring gifts. So giving a gift may be a display of respect or reverence.

When David had conquered the Moabites they "became servants to David and brought tribute" (2 Samuel 8:2). The same is said of the Syrians in 2 Samuel 8:6. So giving a gift may be an expression of submission to the service of a greater power.

Psalm 96 is all about God's authority and control over every aspect of life and in verse 8 His people are called upon to demonstrate that by bringing an offering, a present.

9

When I bring God a gift I am acknowledging His superiority, showing Him respect and reverence, submitting to His service and acknowledging His authority over every aspect of life and that all that I have is from Him.

A Special Significance

In Leviticus 2 there is something more. Three times the phrase "a memorial portion" is used (2, 9, 16). This gift is a reminder of the covenant between God and His people.

In each of these verses the phrase is used to describe the part that is offered to God. Does God need reminding of His covenant? Surely God doesn't forget!

After the flood God admits to being reminded of His covenant with Noah: "When I bring clouds over the earth and the bow is seen in the clouds, I will remember my covenant" (Genesis 9:15-16). When speaking of the New Covenant through the prophet, God says that He will choose to forget: "I will forgive their iniquity, and I will remember their sin no more" (Jeremiah 31:34).

Who can possibly understand how God's memory works? What I am sure of is that we need to be assured that God is not forgetful. Nehemiah needed this assurance. Seven times he called upon God to remember (Nehemiah 1:8; 5:19; 6:14; 13:14, 22, 29, 31).

The offering in Leviticus is certainly a reminder to the worshipper. It is a reminder of his covenant relationship with God. It is a reminder that God has chosen them of all the peoples of the world, that He is Israel's God, that He has promised care, provision and protection. In fact He had promised them His *shalom*, that all-inclusive well-being. As the smoke from the burning portion rose heavenwards, the worshipper was assured that God would not forget.

It is also a reminder to the worshipper of what he owes God. He owes not just a 'portion' of what he brings, not even all of what he brings, but everything he has and is. It is a reminder that if he wishes to enjoy God's *shalom* he has certain obligations: to keep from idolatry, to worship the LORD alone, and to obey God's laws.

The Christian believer's giving is motivated by "the grace of our Lord Jesus Christ" who became poor to make us rich (2 Corinthians 8:9). At the same time, he is aware that however generous he is, it is nothing beside the "inexpressible" generosity of God (2 Corinthians 9:15).

10

No Atonement Here

The fact that this is intended as a gift given by those already in a covenant relationship with God is shown by the fact that there is no use of the word "atonement" here. There is no suggestion that as a result the worshipper will be at one with God. This is not a bribe; this does not form the basis of acceptance by God.

Atonement is made through the shedding of blood.   In Leviticus 1 instructions are given about the burnt offering, of which God says "it shall be accepted for him to make atonement for him" (4). This is followed in Leviticus 2 by the offering of a gift. Atonement is made first then the gift is acceptable.

This was the order that God had commanded. In Exodus 29 Moses is instructed that every day two burnt offerings shall be made, one in the morning and another in the evening. Each one is to be accompanied by a grain offering, a gift. "The other lamb you shall offer at twilight, and shall offer with it a grain offering" (Exodus 29:41). So the burnt offering first for atonement, to establish and confirm the relationship between the worshipper and God, then the gift as an expression of that relationship.

All this is fulfilled in Jesus: "For if the blood of goats and bulls --- sanctify for the purification of the flesh, how much more will the blood of Christ --- purify our conscience from dead works to serve the living God" (Hebrews 9:13-14). So the removal of the sin barrier comes first, followed by the gift, the service. Otherwise it is as the prophet explains, "We have all become like one who is unclean, and all our righteous deeds are like a polluted garment" (Isaiah 64:6).

It is not just a matter of dealing with past sins and covering a sinful nature. The Israelite couldn't say, "It doesn't matter how I live. If I sin I can always offer a burnt offering and my gift will be accepted." God calls His people to holy living.

There is an enormous emphasis on this in Leviticus. The word "holy" is used 92 times; that is nearly as many as in the rest of the Pentateuch (104 times). The words signifying cleanliness are used 187 times in Leviticus but only 50 times altogether in the other four books of the Pentateuch.

There are two sides to becoming holy. "Consecrate yourselves, therefore, and be holy, for I am the LORD your God. Keep my statutes and do them; I am the LORD who sanctifies you." (20:7-8) The Israelites were to "consecrate" themselves by obeying God's laws; God had begun the process of sanctifying them by setting them apart from other nations, by giving them His laws and by coming to dwell among them.

These two parts are necessary for the Christian: "Work out your own salvation with fear and trembling, for it is God who works in you, both to will and to work for his good pleasure." (Philippians 2:12-13)

God's Choice

The fact that obedience is at the heart of holiness is borne out by the fact that God tells His people what to give Him. The giving is voluntary, but it must be what God wants.

In some parts of Christendom it is customary to give things up for Lent. As far as I know it is usually the individual who decides what to give up. But the gift of Leviticus 2 is not like that. Here it is God Who decides what is to be given. "When anyone brings a grain offering as an offering to the LORD, his offering *shall be* of fine flour" and so on. The giving is voluntary, but the gift must be what God wants.

Of course, unlike the gods of the heathen who supposedly actually ate what was given, God doesn't actually need flour and salt and oil. "If I were hungry, I would not tell you, for the world and its fullness are mine" (Psalm 50:12). So why ask for such things?

When we were children my father used to use his hands to make shadows on the wall; shapes of birds, dogs, rabbits. We enjoyed the shadows but they were only shadows; the reality was two hands with fingers and thumbs.

Paul, writing about the ritual law says, "These are a shadow of the things to come, but the substance belongs to Christ" (Colossians 2:17). Paul probably borrowed the illustration from Plato. The difference was that, whereas Plato was saying that the authorities were deliberately keeping the truth from the people by letting them see only shadows of reality, Paul was saying that the shadows of the Old Testament are to help us to know and understand the reality. The reality "belongs to Christ" because He is the complete fulfilment of the shadows. He makes their meaning clear and He calls us to follow Him.

Salt, flour, frankincense and oil are shadows. We have to ask what they illustrate of what Christ requires of those who would follow Him.

12

Salt

"You shall season all your grain offerings with salt. You shall not let *the salt of the covenant with your God* be missing from your grain offering; with all your offerings you shall offer salt" (13).

In the past, salt was hard to get and hence of great value, so sharing it was a great favour. Up until 50 or 60 years ago certainly, and maybe still today, if an Arab shared his salt with you, even if only as a symbolic sprinkle, it showed that you had been welcomed as if a member of the tribe and you could be sure of the tribe's care and protection. Equally, by accepting the salt you would take on the responsibility of being loyal to the tribe.

God made "a covenant of salt" with Aaron that all the contributions made by the people of Israel were to be for Aaron and his descendants for all time (Numbers 18:19). God made "a covenant of salt" with David and his descendants concerning the kingship (2 Chronicles 13:5).

The salt in the gift was to be not only a reminder of the covenant between God and Israel, but also a reaffirmation of commitment to it.

Jesus, as He shared the wine at the Last Supper said, "This cup that is poured out for you is the new covenant in my blood" (Luke 22:20). Accepting the wine at communion is not only a reminder of that new covenant, but is also a reaffirmation of one's commitment to both its benefits and its responsibilities. It is only within that covenant relationship that anything offered is acceptable to God.

Fine flour

"When anyone brings a grain offering as an offering to the LORD, his offering shall be of fine flour." (1)

Fine flour was produced by removing the husk and the germ, then grinding the kernels down to the finest powder. It was flour in which there were absolutely no impurities at all. It was perfect.

Jesus said, "You must be perfect, as your heavenly Father is perfect" (Matthew 5:48). He was talking about loving, that is, meeting the needs of others at whatever the cost to oneself. He said that that loving care must be shown, not only to friends but also to enemies. He called for acting in a loving, caring way to others regardless of how they behave.

Our Heavenly Father loves like that: "While we were enemies we were reconciled to God by the death of his Son" (Romans 5:10). Those who would follow Jesus must do the same. Paul said, "Love is the fulfilling of the law" (Romans 13:10).

Frankincense

Burning the toast doesn't give off a particularly pleasing smell. That would apply to the grain offering. So the portion that is burnt on the altar is to have frankincense on it.

The frankincense referred to here is a product of certain trees which grow in south Arabia and Somaliland (see Jeremiah 6:20). The gum, which is obtained by incising the bark, is ground to a powder. It was to be one of four constituents of the incense for use exclusively in the worship of God (Exodus 30:34-38). When burnt, frankincense emits a fragrant smell and thus the "memorial portion" would present "a pleasing aroma to the LORD". (2, 9, 12)

Paul wrote, "We are the aroma of Christ to God among those who are being saved and among those who are perishing, to one a fragrance from death to death, to the other a fragrance from life to life" (2 Corinthians 2:15-16). If our lives are a demonstration of love for God and impartial, loving care for others, then our lives will be "the aroma of Christ to God". Notice that it is to God. Sometimes as Christians we are too concerned about what the world thinks of us. For some unbelievers, what is a pleasing fragrance to God, is the smell of death to them and confirms them in their downhill path. To others it is an encouragement to give themselves to Christ and live.

Oil

Oil was always to be included whether the gift was of uncooked fine flour (1), or baked in an oven (4), or baked on a griddle (5), or cooked in a pan (7), or a gift of first-fruits (14-16).

Oil often symbolises the work of the Holy Spirit. It is by the Spirit of God that we are able to produce the fruit of the Spirit, to live God-pleasing lives (Galatians 5:22-23). It is by the Spirit of God that we are able to serve God beyond the limits of our natural talents.

Moses was given the task of building the Tabernacle and its furniture. Those who would do the work had been slaves and were the descendants of slaves. How could they possibly do the skilled work required? God reassures Moses with the promise, "See, I have called by name Bezalel the son of Uri, son of Hur, of the tribe of Judah, and I have filled him with the Spirit of God, with ability and intelligence, with knowledge and all craftsmanship, to devise

14

artistic designs, to work in gold, silver, and bronze, in cutting stones for setting, and in carving wood, to work in every craft" (Exodus 31:2-5).

After the Israelites returned from exile in Babylon, their leader, Zerubbabel had the task of rebuilding the Temple in the face of great opposition. But God gave Zechariah a vision of a lampstand with an olive tree on each side giving a continuous supply of oil to the lamp. And the message to Zerubbabel from God was, "Not by might, nor by power, but by my Spirit, says the LORD of hosts" (Zechariah 4:6). The Spirit of God would enable him to overcome every difficulty.

It has been said in recent years that what the Church needs more than anything in these days are *genuine* spiritual gifts (1 Corinthians 12:11).

Nothing can be done that is acceptable to God without the enabling of the Holy Spirit.

Prohibitions

Yeast and honey are forbidden without any reason being given (11). The symbolic significance of this prohibition may be because they promote decay and have the opposite effect to that of salt.

Or it may be because they figured hugely in heathen sacrifices. Perhaps this is a shadow of what Paul writes about not being "conformed to this world" (Romans 12:2). It is so easy for us to allow our opinions and attitudes to be formed by what we hear or read in the media, by what experts pronounce. We need to submit our minds to the renewing work of the Holy Spirit working through God's Word.

Building God's Kingdom

What was not burnt was food for the priests: "The rest of the grain offering shall be for Aaron and his sons" (3&10). In this way, by giving to God the worshipper was enabling the service of God in the Tabernacle to continue.

When the Israelites entered the Promised Land, a portion of the land was allotted to each tribe except the tribe of Levi. The descendants of Levi, including the descendants of Aaron, the priests, were dispersed throughout the land and were maintained through the offerings made at the Tabernacle and eventually at the Temple. This, as already mentioned, was the "covenant of salt" which God made with Aaron and his descendants for all time (Numbers 18:19).

And it is evident from Scriptures such as Deuteronomy 27&28 and the book of Ezra, that the guarding of the Law and its teaching became the responsibility of the Levites. So that by giving to God the worshipper was helping to maintain not only the rituals of the sanctuary but also the work of God in keeping the people faithful to Him.

The significance for us is obvious. In giving our money, our time and our God-given talents in supporting the activities of the church we help maintain the work of God. But the meetings and activities come to an end, and we leave the church building to disperse into the community where we spend most of our time. What then?

The growing of the grain, the preparation of flour and the cooking of bread were everyday activities for the Israelites. And in Leviticus 2 God asks for a gift, not from "religious activities" but from their everyday, workaday lives.

In our homes and out in the community, as we fulfil God's law by practising impartial love, as we bear the fruit of the Spirit, as we combat lies with the truth of the Gospel, indeed as we give our whole lives to Him we are playing our part in maintaining and promoting the work of God's Kingdom.

The Peace Offering
Leviticus 3:1-17 and 7:11-18

Sharing a meal with family and friends seems to be a universal way of celebrating on occasions such as birthdays, weddings and Christmas. Even when there is no special event or festival to celebrate, to invite others to share a meal or to be invited oneself is an indication of acceptance and real fellowship.

The peace offering culminated in a meal (Leviticus 7) which the worshipper shared with family, friends, neighbours and servants (Deuteronomy 12:7&12). For this reason it is sometimes referred to as "the fellowship offering", "the communion offering" or "the shared offering". Since the derivation of the word translated "peace" is uncertain, such names may help to fill out the meaning that word is intended to convey. But the meal is not mentioned until Leviticus 7, and then not as a command to eat but as a restriction on how long the meal should last or be delayed.

Why is that? Although the meal was the intended climax of the peace offering, there were some things which had to be attended to first. Those things were more important than the meal itself since without them the meal would lose its significance and would become no more than an opportunity for self-indulgence.

A Blood Sacrifice

It is obvious that the peace offering was not simply the butchering of an animal in preparation for a feast. It was a blood sacrifice.

The actions required of the worshipper were exactly the same as the burnt offering. He had to bring the animal to the entrance, lay his hand on its head and kill it (3:2). He had to skin and butcher it (3:3&4). The priests had to perform the same tasks as for the burnt offering. They had to throw the blood against the sides of the altar (3:2) and arrange the required parts of the animal on the altar to be burnt (3:5).

So this was at least a reminder of the need for atonement and that atonement is achieved by the shedding of blood (17:11). This is emphasised by the fact that the peace offering was to be burnt "on top of the burnt offering" (3:5). Whether that was to be a burnt offering offered by the same worshipper or whether it could be one of the two daily burnt offerings is not clear, but it is

17

The Sin Offering
Leviticus 4:1 to 5:13

Sin, it seems, isn't sin any longer. Behaviour that was frowned upon fifty years ago and only spoken of in whispers is now accepted. Sexual deviance that was treated as a crime is now celebrated and encouraged. A recent article argued that a young man who had committed murder should not be blamed because his action was the result of the way his father had treated him.

However, in God's eyes sin is serious because the sinner is opposing himself to God and His will (Romans 5:10). Sin creates a barrier between man and God (Isaiah 59:2), who is the source of life (Psalm 36:9). Sin enslaves (Romans 6:17) and it pollutes the world, affecting all around and not just the sinner himself (18:24-25).

The Seriousness of Sin

According to the Old Testament law, for adultery and sexual deviance (20:10-21), for blasphemy (24:16) and for murder (35:31), the offender is to be 'put to death'. For sins committed 'with a high hand', that is those that are planned and premeditated and of which the sinner is aware and is in deliberate defiance of God's laws (Numbers 15:30-31) the offender will be 'cut off'. For such sins there was no atonement, no forgiveness.

David, guilty of adultery with Bathsheba and the murder of her husband, appealed (Psalm 51) to God's amazing grace and mercy (Exodus 34:7). But the pronouncement of God through the prophet Nathan was that 'the sword would never depart' from David's house (2 Samuel 12:10), and that the child born to Bathsheba would die (2 Samuel 12:14). That judgment was carried through.

Even failure to observe the cleansing rituals, for instance after touching a dead body, would result in 'the tabernacle of the LORD' being defiled, and the offender being 'cut off from Israel' (Numbers 19:13).

The consequence of sin is death (Genesis 2:17; Ezekiel 18:4). This was not always immediate and obvious, but for God's people to survive, atonement and forgiveness had to be provided. God did that for His people in the sin offering.

24

Unintentional sin

The sin offering was provided for those who sinned unintentionally (4:2). Every action is the result of a decision, the will is involved, so every sin is a matter of choice. Is it possible to sin unintentionally?

Examples of unintentional sin are detailed in 5:1-4. The first example is of failing to speak up against wrong. The second is of failing to take care to avoid touching something that is unclean as defined by the Law. The last is of making a 'rash' vow which, when it comes to it, proves to be impossible to keep. It is a matter of speaking when it would have been better to remain silent.

In setting out the laws for guilt offerings unintentional sin is described as a "mistake" (5:18). Such sins are the result of human weakness and of carelessness, rather than of any deliberate disobedience. This understanding of "unintentionally" is borne out by the root meaning of the Hebrew word which is "to wander" or "to err". It refers to sins which the sinner, through human weakness, was unable to prevent himself from committing.

However, neither ignorance nor weakness is an excuse. Atonement must be made, forgiveness is necessary.

Forgiveness

The statement that "the priest shall make atonement for him/them, and he/they shall be forgiven" is made four times in Leviticus 4 (20, 26, 31 and 35) and twice in Leviticus 5 (10 and 13).

The fact that forgiveness is in mind is shown in the details of the procedure that this offering has in common with those of the burnt offering and the peace offering. The worshipper was to bring the animal to the entrance, lay his hand on its head and kill it. He was identifying with an animal that was to die as a substitute in his place. The punishment due to him was borne by another and he was forgiven.

All this was to be done "before the LORD" as in the burnt offering and the peace offering. The fat as specified for the peace offering was burnt on the altar. The sacrifice was being made to God; the price required was paid; God was satisfied; forgiveness was granted.

This is emphasised by the fact that with the sacrifices for priest and for congregation it is explicitly stated that the remains of the animal were to be taken outside the camp and burnt. The sin was removed completely, the record wiped clean.

Atonement

The statement "the priest shall make atonement for him/them, and he/they shall be forgiven" seems to indicate that there is more to atonement than forgiveness, vitally important though that is.

There are details in the procedures prescribed for the sin offering that are quite different from those for the burnt offering and the peace offering. These are in the way the blood is dealt with.

The blood of the burnt offering and of the peace offering was thrown against the sides of the altar of burnt offering (1:5; 3:2) which was near the entrance to the tent of meeting. But in the sin offering the blood ritual varies according to the status of the sinner.

The reason for the differences in the rituals is that sin pollutes. The sins of the nations of Canaan had made the land unclean so that God 'punished its iniquity, and the land vomited out its inhabitants' (18:24-25). Even when the sin involved was the failure to carry out ritual cleansing by one of God's people, it polluted, and what it polluted was God's sanctuary (Numbers 19:13). Sin by God's people defiled God's sanctuary, "the tabernacle of the LORD". The purpose of the sin offering was not only to secure forgiveness but to cleanse. The blood, as the "disinfectant", had to be applied to those parts of the tabernacle visited by the sinner. So the application of the blood varied according to the identity of the offender.

The rules to be followed when the offender is a priest are given in 4:3-12. The phrase "the anointed priest" (4:3) has been taken to mean the High Priest. But all the priests were anointed (Exodus 30:30 and Leviticus 10:6-7) and if only the High Priest is intended here, other priests seem not to have been catered for in the sin offering. Perhaps the priest is referred to in this way to emphasise the seriousness of his offense.

The priest had to follow the same initial procedures as for others. He started at the entrance (4:4). There was no fast-tracking him just because he was a priest. Having placed his hands on the animal's head he killed it, as did other worshippers. But from then on the ritual was specially designed for him. The priest was in a very special position in the community. His task was to represent the people before God. Whatever his sin it would render him

26

unacceptable in God's presence. His performance of the rituals would be contaminated, and thus ineffective, and the people would in effect be shut off from God. More than that, his sin would defile the places where he performed the rituals. So the blood had to be applied in the Holy Place, on the altar of incense and on, or in front, of the veil.

Similarly but figuratively, the whole congregation (4:13) "entered" the Holy Place when the priest entered as their representative. So, for the sin offering, the blood was applied to the same places as for the priest (4:18).

On the other hand, individuals, whether a leader or one of the common people, never went nearer the presence of God than to the altar of burnt offering, so the blood was applied to the horns of that altar (4:25,30).

Whoever was the offender, the remainder of the blood was poured out at the base of the altar of burnt offering since everybody began their approach to God there.

In these ways the pollution due to sin was cleansed from God's sanctuary.

The Offerings

These differences in the application of the blood were made according to the status of the offender, and hence to the extent of the possible pollution, rather than according to the seriousness of the sin. The same concern is shown in the value of the offering required.

The failure of the priest was not private; as already noted, it affected the whole community by defiling the Holy Place. This was very serious. So the required sacrifice of a bull without blemish (4:3) was in effect the most expensive of all since one man had to meet the whole cost.

For similar reasons a bull was required of the whole congregation (4:14).

A leader would be a tribal chief and would, by his leadership, have an effect on the members of the tribe by example and by giving directions. A male goat without blemish was required of him (4:23).

The influence and polluting potential of one of the common people would be limited in most cases to family and friends. He would be required to bring a female goat or a female lamb (4:28 and 32). If he could not afford a female goat or a female lamb he could offer two turtledoves or two pigeons (5:7). If he could not afford them he could offer a tenth of an ephah of fine flour (5:11). A tenth of an ephah of flour would weigh about three kilos.

The Guilt Offering
Leviticus 5:14 to 6:7

My parents taught me not to get into debt. My aging memory tells me that they often did this but it may have been only a few times. My parents were Christians who knew the Bible very well and they gave me the advice by quoting Paul's words, "Owe no man anything" (Romans 13:8).

The guilt offering is all about being "in debt" and what needs to be done about that.

The burnt offering deals with sin as a barrier between man and God which needs to be removed. When that is done gifts to God become acceptable (the grain offering), and fellowship with God and others becomes possible (the peace offering).

The sin offering treats sin as pollution which requires cleansing.

The guilt offering approaches sin as a debt that must be paid with interest.

The Sins Dealt With

The sins for which this offering is prescribed are identified by a word in 5:15 and 6:2 which specifies a particular kind of sin. That word refers to an invasion of the rights of others, especially in matters of property or of services due. Some English versions use the word "trespass".

The word also implies an abuse of the trust put in one not to cross accepted boundaries. Other English versions express this concept by using the phrase "a breach of faith" or words and phrases that convey the idea of being unfaithful.

These concepts are illustrated in some of the circumstances in which the word is used.

In Numbers 5:12 it is used to refer to adultery - an act of taking and giving what belongs to another and of being unfaithful. In Joshua 7:1 it is used of Achan's sin when he took from Jericho items which were "devoted to the LORD for destruction". It is used of idolatry in 2 Chronicles 29:6 - giving to idols the service which belongs to God.

The result of trespassing and breaking faith is that the offender is guilty (5:17&19; 6:4&5). The Hebrew word used here denotes being legally guilty. The guilt is objective not just a feeling. The offender is guilty according to God's law. The rituals and requirements of the guilt offering are designed to deal with that guilt.

The guilt offering was not available to Achan because he sinned deliberately and failed to admit his fault until found out. Because of that he suffered the ultimate penalty for sin. The guilt offering was given by God to bring relief from the guilt of sins committed unintentionally (5:15&18), or for occasions when the sinner only later "realizes his guilt" (6:4&5), owns up and seeks to put matters right.

Definite Offences against God

Leviticus 5:15 refers to sins which involve "the holy things of the LORD".

These holy things include anything to do with the tabernacle, its furniture and utensils and the offerings made there. Other things that were due to God, or dedicated to Him voluntarily were also "holy things". Sinning in these things would mean using any of these things for oneself or failing to give God what was rightfully His.

An example is given in 22:14 where it speaks of someone eating "of a holy thing". A firstborn animal was God's (Exodus 34:19), therefore "a holy thing". Eating its meat by mistake would incur guilt. The same would be true of eating the first-fruits of harvest (Exodus 23:19).

Another possibility concerns the tithe. One tenth of all possessions belonged to God (27:30-33), it was holy. If a man used his possessions to benefit himself and then found he could not pay the tithe, he would be guilty of a trespass, a breach of faith.

It was God's due that vows should be paid. A man or woman could make a vow, the Nazirite vow (Numbers 6:1-21), to dedicate themselves completely to God for a certain period of time. If that vow was broken, for instance by touching a dead body, even though it was that of a close relative, a guilt offering was required (Numbers 6:12).

Cases of Uncertainty

Leviticus 5:17-19 seems to be dealing with an instance where the worshipper feels guilty but is unsure about exactly what he has done. This is indicated by the use of the phrase "though he did not know it", by the very general definition "doing any of the things that by the LORD's commandments ought not to be done" and by the fact that no restitution is required since the offence is unknown and so is impossible to value.

In spite of all that, his conscience is not misleading him, "he has indeed incurred guilt before the LORD" and a guilt offering is required.

Offences against One's Neighbour

Leviticus 6:1-7 deals with trespassing on the property rights of others and being unreliable and unfaithful in promises and deals. Examples of this are misusing something entrusted to one for safe-keeping; giving as security what is worthless; taking possession of something with insufficient or no payment; mistreating servants or withholding their wages; finding and keeping what belongs to another.

Linked in with this is the offence of "swearing falsely" (6:3&5). When brought before the judges the offender has sworn before God that he is innocent.

None of these things could be done unintentionally and that condition is not mentioned here. With any of these offences, if he "has realized his guilt" (6:4) and restores in full what he owes "and shall add a fifth to it" (6:5), he may then make a guilt offering and "the priest shall make atonement for him before the LORD, and he shall be forgiven" (6:7).

So it seems that atonement for a deliberate sin was possible when true repentance was shown by remorse ("realized his guilt") and restitution.

The Offering

Whatever the offence the offering required was the same, "a ram without blemish out of the flock" (5:15, 6:6). It had to be without defect and a domestic animal, not one caught in the wild. So it would be costly.

Its value was to be determined "according to the shekel of the sanctuary". The restitution made had to be measured, not by human standards, but by that of God. The priest would determine its value and decide if its value fitted the offence.

Alternatively the offender could bring "its equivalent" (5:18, 6:6). This equivalent in silver would have to be used to purchase a ram of appropriate value since, in God's instructions to the priests (7:1-5) the guilt offering had to be killed, its blood thrown against the sides of the altar and its fat, kidneys and liver burnt "as a food offering to the LORD".

Whatever the offence, the same offering was required because, even in the matter of an offence against the property or rights of others, it was "against the LORD" (6:1).

Sin is always an offence against God, its penalty is death and there is only one way for the guilt to be removed. In a passage in Numbers 5 where the need for a guilt offering is reiterated, it is explained that the offender is required to "confess his sin" (6:7). Confession of sin was done when the offender identified with the animal by placing his hand on its head. As with

34

other blood sacrifices, the ram of the guilt offering died in the offender's place and atonement was made by substitution.

Restitution

However, in God's instructions through Moses to the offender none of these details are mentioned. What is emphasised is the need to repay what has been wrongly taken and to add a fifth to that as compensation (5:16, 6:4&5).

Rams were used for paying debts in Bible times. There is an example of this in 2 Chronicles 17:11. The ram of the guilt offering was repayment to God for what He was owed (5:16, 6:6) and a fifth of its value was to be added to that, presumably in silver shekels. Restitution was to be made to God whether the offence was against "the holy things" or against a fellow Israelite. Both were equally an offence against God (6:2).

If the offence involved the property or rights of another person, restoration had to be made in full. A fifth of the value of the offence had to be added to that so that not even a temporary advantage would be gained from doing wrong. This was to be done "on the day he realizes his guilt" (6:5) and only then could he bring the ram for the guilt offering. The guilt offering was not acceptable unless true repentance had been demonstrated by making restitution. On the other hand, making restitution was not enough, the guilt before God must also be dealt with.

It is worth noting that if the offender was found guilty on the basis of another's evidence, he had to repay double (Exodus 22:9). But if the offender realised his guilt and sought to make amends without being brought to court, he had to add only one fifth.

Fulfilment

While, "It is impossible for the blood of bulls and goats to take away sins" (Hebrews 10:4), the good news is that, as already noted, the Old Testament rituals "are a shadow of the things to come, but the substance belongs to Christ" (Colossians 2:17). So we can confidently expect that, as with the other sacrifices, there will be a clear fulfilment of the guilt offering in Jesus.

At the Last Supper, the Lord Jesus, as He tried to prepare His disciples for what was soon to happen to Him at Calvary, quoted Isaiah 53:12, "I tell you that this Scripture must be fulfilled in me: 'And he was numbered with the transgressors.'" (Luke 22:37)

So we can be confident that Isaiah 53 is fulfilled in Jesus. Just as the Suffering Servant was to be God's provision for the sin offering, so He was to be the fulfilment of the guilt offering. In verse 10, when the prophet speaks of the Suffering Servant making his soul "an offering for sin", he uses the same word as is used for the guilt offering in Leviticus 5 & 6.

35

The guilt offering treats sin as a debt that must be paid.

Jesus taught His disciples to pray, "Forgive us our debts" (Matthew 6:12). When a sinful woman anointed Jesus' feet and Simon the Pharisee disapproved, Jesus told a parable about two debtors and equated the cancelling of their debts with being forgiven (Luke 7:36-50). In the parable of the unforgiving servant, the story revolves around the forgiving of debt, and Jesus said that the kingdom of heaven is like that (Matthew 18:21-35).

Because of our sin we owe God a debt which we can never repay. But Jesus paid that debt for us.

Paul explained the death of Jesus as being payment of the debt we owe God when he wrote that God has forgiven us, "by cancelling the record of debt that stood against us with its legal demands. This he set aside, nailing it to the cross." (Colossians 2:13-14)

The cost of the guilt offering to the offender in Old Testament times was substantial. The cost of God's Great Guilt Offering was the life of His Son. But it costs the offender nothing; in His grace God has paid it all.

A Reasonable Response

But accepting God's grace doesn't come cheaply. The Gospel does not proclaim "easy believism"; it is not simply a matter of "believe in Jesus and you'll be forgiven and go to heaven." Accepting God's grace is costly because it demands denying oneself, taking up the cross and following Christ (Matthew 16:24).

The requirement to love God "with all your heart and with all your soul and with all your mind" (Matthew 22:37) still stands. In fact, as Jesus made clear in the Sermon on the Mount, particularly in a series of sayings which begin with, "You have heard that it was said ..." and conclude with, "But I say to you ...", God's requirements go far beyond the usual understanding of what the Old Testament moral law requires.

The "holy things" of God mentioned in Leviticus 5 were objects and vows which were distinct from the common run of everyday life. But Christians are "called to be saints" (Romans 1:7), that is, called to be set apart, to be holy. Moreover, we are not our own, we have been "bought with a price" (1 Corinthians 6:19, 20). All that I have and am, my possessions and abilities, my words and deeds and even my thoughts are God's "holy things", set apart for His use. This, Paul wrote, is a reasonable response (Romans 12:1-2) to all that God has done for me.

When I use these things for my own benefit or pleasure, even though it may be unintentionally, I need to go back to the Cross to seek forgiveness. Not only that, in the terms of this Guilt Offering as with the old one, where possible I need to make amends, I need to put things right and give God His due.

The Social Dimension

Often, in failing to give God His due, the rights of others are violated.

A major concern of politicians these days is the matter of human rights and who makes and upholds the laws governing those rights. On the other hand, it has been decided that the matter of God's rights has no place in politics. While the latter is deplorable, God Himself takes a deep interest in human rights as 6:1-7 for example makes clear.

It remains the rightful concern of Christians also. The verse my parents quoted in giving advice about debt reads in full, "Owe no one anything, except to love each other, for the one who loves another has fulfilled the law" (Romans 13:8). Giving God His due by fulfilling the law includes giving others what is due to them by loving them.

In these days, it is probably a good idea to remind ourselves occasionally what is meant by the love God has shown for us and which He expects from us in return. This love is not merely a feeling but is always expressed in action. God expressed His love for the world by giving His Son (John 3:16). The Son of God "loved me and gave Himself for me" (Galatians 2:20). John wrote, "If anyone has the world's goods and sees his brother in need, yet closes his heart against him, how does God's love abide in him? Little children, let us not love in word or talk but in deed and in truth." (1 John 3:17-18) The kind of concern for human rights that God looks for in us is not only to refrain from wronging another, but to reach out to meet the needs of others as we are able. We owe them this.

The law of 6:1-7 required that restitution should be made for wrong done. Jesus recognised that the desire to make amends is an indication that God is doing a saving work in the offender's life. When Zacchaeus met Jesus he declared that he would give half his goods to the poor and would restore four times over anything that he had taken wrongly. Jesus responded, "Today salvation has come to this house" (Luke 19:9).

If there is no desire to make restitution it is doubtful if God really is at work in a person's life since one's relationship with God is affected by one's relationship with others. Jesus taught us to pray, "Forgive us our debts as we forgive our debtors", and He followed that with the warning that those who fail to forgive others will not experience God's forgiveness (Matthew 6:9-15). Under the terms of the guilt offering, the offender was required to make restitution before bringing the ram for a guilt offering. Jesus said, "If you are offering your gift at the altar and there remember that your brother has something against you, leave your gift there before the altar and go. First be reconciled to your brother, and then come and offer your gift." (Matthew 5:23-24) Engaging in acts of worship is no substitute for paying one's dues, for repairing relationships.

This is personal

The sin offering made provision for sin committed by "the whole congregation of Israel" (4:13). Since, in this case, it was the elders of the congregation who were required to lay their hands on the sacrificial animal, (4:15) it would seem that the nation had been led astray by their leaders.

No provision is made for such sins in the rules for the guilt offering. Each part of God's instructions for this offering begins with "If anyone..." and each concluding assurance includes the statement "he shall be forgiven". Guilt is a matter for the individual.

There is no such thing as a Christian nation. It is for each individual to confess their sins, repent and accept Christ as their own, personal Guilt Offering.

It is possible for an individual to do something for which there is no specific prohibition in Scripture, yet a feeling of guilt results and the conscience is troubled. The solution is to take the directions of 5:17-19 as a guide, to go to the Cross, repent and confess, and rest in the fact that, through God's Guilt Offering, atonement has been made and forgiveness is assured.

Jesus has paid the debt each individual owes to God. In response, God requires that each one should give the love that they owe to Him and to others.

Instructions to Priests

Leviticus 6:8 to 7:38

This passage concludes God's instructions for the five types of offering which He required from His people (7:37-38). In instructions given previously Moses is told, "Speak to the people of Israel" (1:2; 4:2), but this passage begins, "Command Aaron and his sons" (6:9). There is some repetition here but it is made only in order to present new instructions which particularly concern the priests.

The priests were specially ordained and wore special clothes as later chapters show. Dressed in their finery they would have looked very grand. They would have been held in high esteem by the common people. But in these verses God makes it clear that they are His servants and must carry out their duties exactly as He requires.

The Burnt Offering (6:8-13)

The offering referred to here is that described in Exodus 29:38-42. One lamb was to be offered in the morning. Everything else burnt on the altar during the day would be placed on top of that first lamb. At the end of the day the second lamb would be offered and burnt and would be there all night. The burnt offering was to be continuous.

To achieve this, the fire must be kept burning. "Fire shall be kept burning on the altar continually; it shall not go out" (6:12-13). So instructions for renewing the wood and removing the ashes are given.

God made himself known to Moses by fire in the Burning Bush (Exodus 3:2). He descended onto Mount Sinai in fire (Exodus 19:18). His presence in the tabernacle was shown by fire at night (Exodus 40:38). He led the people at night during their time in the wilderness by a pillar of fire (Exodus 13:21-22). Fire would, therefore, have been a symbol to the Israelites of the presence of God. The continuous burnt offering would be a perpetual reminder that, for God to continue dwelling with them, atonement was constantly required.

Entitlements

The priest who offers any burnt offering "shall have for himself the skin of the burnt offering" (7:8). He is also entitled to eat the meat from the sin offering provided its blood had not been sprinkled in the sanctuary (6:25-30). The meat from the guilt offering is to be given to the officiating priest (7:7), as is the right thigh of the peace offering (7:32-33). He is also to be given any grain offering that has been cooked (7:9), and one of each type of loaf that accompanies the peace offering (7:14).

Some food from the offerings is to be given to the priests as a group. Grain offerings that consist of flour "shall be shared equally among all the sons of Aaron" (7:10). The breast from the peace offering shall also be "for Aaron and his sons" (7:31).

So God gives exact details about how the food is to be distributed and he makes it clear in 7:34-36 that these arrangements are permanent. From now on there should be no disagreements or quarrelling about who has the right to this or that. All they have to do is to obey.

This is emphasized by the requirement to "wave" the breast from the peace offering. The worshipper is to "bring the fat with the breast" (7:29-30). The fat is for God alone (3:17) and the breast is brought "to the LORD" with the fat. So the breast also belongs to God. Then the breast is "waved", it is held up towards the Holy Place and presented to God. Only then is it given to the priests. So the priests are always reminded that the breast and, indeed, all the food they have is not theirs by right but by God's gracious provision.

Limitations

This passage is not only about the entitlements of priests. God also gave commands which place limitations on what was permissible. The reason for these is not always clear.

On the day that a priest was anointed for service he offered a sacrifice which he would repeat every morning and every evening during his service as priest. It was to be a grain offering (6:20). But, unlike the grain offering of a lay person, it was not to be eaten but was to be completely burned (6:22-23). His offering to God would be meaningless if he profited from it himself.

The reasons for the ban on eating fat or blood (3:17; 7:23-27) are clear. The fat belonged to God alone (3:16). The purpose of blood was to make atonement for their souls (17:10-11) and was to be kept solely for that purpose. To eat it, for instance in meat that had not been drained of blood, would be to reduce its sacred importance in the minds of the Israelites and the blood rituals involved in the sacrifices would lose their impact. It is for a similar reason that blood splashed on a garment was to be washed off "in a holy place" (6:27), that is, within the confines of the tabernacle court.

Vessels used to cook the flesh of the sin offering were to be broken if earthenware, or scoured and rinsed with water if bronze (6:28). This may be that, because the sin of the worshipper had been placed upon the animal, for the sin to be dealt with, not the slightest trace of the "tainted" offering must remain.

With the greater seriousness of sin by a priest or the nation as a whole, the flesh was completely burned (6:30); none of it was to be eaten. Once again, not the slightest trace must remain.

The meat from a peace offering for thanksgiving was to be eaten on the day of the sacrifice (7:15). It has been suggested that this was in order to encourage sharing with as many as possible to avoid waste. The reason for allowing the feasting to continue for a second day after peace offerings for a vow or as a freewill offering (7:16) is not clear.

Other questions remain. Why did the priest have to change his clothes (6:10-11)? Why was eating the flesh of a peace offering on the third day such a serious matter (7:17-18)? Why are the grain, sin and guilt offerings and the meat from them referred to as "most holy" (6:17), but the peace offering is not?

Holiness

The answers to these and similar questions depend on an understanding of the meaning of holiness in the Old Testament and its significance in Leviticus.

God commanded Aaron, "You are to distinguish between the holy and the common, and between the unclean and the clean." (10:10)

Everything was to be treated as either holy or common. To be holy in this context means to be set especially apart in accordance with God's commands and instructions for God's particular use. What is common has not been set apart in that way. The tabernacle and its furniture, the sacrifices offered there, and the priests were all holy in that sense.

Everything common was either clean or unclean. The people of Israel and the things of everyday life were common. The people of Israel were to be holy because God is holy (11:44, 45). They were to be holy in the sense that they were to keep themselves separate from anything that would make them unclean. Examples of this were touching a dead body (11:24), skin diseases (13:1 to 14:57), bodily discharges (15:1-33) and committing adultery (18:20). It

41

was the responsibility of Aaron and his successors to maintain these distinctions. Aaron is told, "You are to teach the people of Israel all the statutes that the LORD has spoken to them by Moses." (10:11)

The Hebrew word translated "distinguish" is translated in Genesis 1:6 as "separate". Aaron's responsibility was not only to maintain the doctrine but also to make sure it was followed in practice. He was to keep the holy separate from the common and especially from what was unclean.

Practical Application

The food from the grain offering, the sin offering and the guilt offering is described as "most holy" (6:17&29; 7:6) because this food may be eaten only by the priests, that is, by "holy" people. It must be eaten in "a holy place, in the court of the tent of meeting" (6:26). The meat from the peace offering is not described in that way because it may be eaten by lay people who are "common".

The ashes from the altar of burnt offering are from God's holy fire and God's holy sacrifices. So removing the ashes from the altar is a holy task, and the priest must wear holy garments. But when he leaves the sanctuary with the ashes he must wear ordinary clothes to move through common territory. Holy garments must not be devalued.

The ashes are holy. They must be left in a clean place. They must not be dumped, for instance on a dunghill or where animal remains have been buried.

The flesh of a peace offering left into the third day "is tainted" (7:18). The basic idea of the Hebrew word is that the meat stinks. Without modern-day refrigeration the meat would be beginning to go off. Although possibly still edible it would be unclean and not fit to be eaten at a feast held in the presence of God. The offence is so serious that the sacrifice that has been offered is made unacceptable if that meat is eaten.

Flesh that even touches an unclean thing is rendered unclean itself and so must be burned completely (7:19).

Anyone who is ceremonially unclean is barred from eating at the feast of a peace offering because God is there (7:20-21).

Uncleanness is incompatible with the presence of God. The distinctions between holy and common, clean and unclean must be maintained.

A Serious Matter

Keeping the unclean and the holy separate was very important for the individual. For instance, "The person who eats of the flesh of the sacrifice of the LORD's peace offerings while an uncleanness is on him, that person shall be cut off from his people."(7:20). It is not clear exactly what being "cut off" means. It might mean that there would be no further offspring, so that the family line would end there. It might mean that the offender would die by an act of God.

It was deadly serious for the nation. In a vision given to Ezekiel to explain the reason for the exile, he is shown God's once holy temple full of idolatry and related, obnoxious things (Ezekiel 8 and 9). Then he is shown the glory of God leaving the temple (Ezekiel 10). God had departed from his temple because it had been defiled and the nation was left unprotected, vulnerable to the attacks of their enemies.

Fellowship Maintained

Although the holy and the common must be kept separate, God wants fellowship with His people. This is clearly shown in His provision of the sacrifices.

The priests were made holy in accordance with rituals commanded by God. They received the sacrifices from the people and presented them to God. They met the people at the entrance to the tabernacle court and they entered the holy place. On the Day of Atonement the high priest, on behalf of the people, entered the most holy place where God dwelt. So the priesthood, working through the tabernacle court, functioned as a sort of airlock, keeping holy and common separate, but, at the same time, providing a means of communication between the two.

Simple Obedience

Several of the explanations given here are surmise. Even Aaron and his sons may not have completely understood the reason for some of these instructions. The fact that the directions are given in great detail and without complete explanation emphasises the need to obey God because He is God.

The great apostle Paul introduced himself as "a servant of Christ Jesus" (Romans 1:1) and referred to other church leaders in the same way (Romans 16:1; Colossians 4:12). As God's servants, church leaders are to be concerned, not with their own authority or reputation but to do God's will.

43

This is true for all of us, not only for leaders. Real worship and service mean submitting oneself to God in body and mind in order to discern His will and put it into practice (Romans 12:1-2). To love God means obeying Him because He is God even when we don't understand.

Orderly worship

The worship required by God was not something done at the last minute without thought or preparation or at the personal preference of the worshipper or the priest. That would seem to lack spirituality to some in these days, but it was what God required.

In the church in Corinth, where spiritual gifts were in plentiful supply (1 Corinthians 1:7), it was necessary for Paul to urge that "all things should be done decently and in order" (1 Corinthians 14:40). The same thought is repeated in Hebrews 12:28-29: "Let us offer to God acceptable worship, with reverence and awe, for our God is a consuming fire."

Even the fellowship meals of the peace offerings were subject to certain rules if they were to be acceptable to God. They could be carefree if carelessness was avoided.

Keeping the Fire Burning

The presence of God was made known to the Israelites by fire. The priests had to ensure that the fire on the altar of burnt offering was never allowed to go out (6:12-13).

When God the Holy Spirit came to dwell in the Church at Pentecost He came as tongues of fire (Acts 2:1-4). The apostles had the responsibility of maintaining the fire by preaching and teaching the truths of the Gospel, that God's presence with His people is on the basis of Christ's sacrifice of Himself. That responsibility falls to church leaders today.

He is the Spirit of Truth (John 16:13). They must ensure that sound doctrine is taught (1Timothy 1:3).

He is Love (1 John 4:8). They must preach and teach in a way that is appropriate to the needs of the people in their charge (Jude 22-23).

In Paul's final list of instructions to the church in Thessalonica he writes, "Do not quench the Spirit" (1 Thessalonians 5:19). His presence and enabling is needed in every activity of the church.

At Pentecost the tongues of fire "rested on each of them" (Acts 2:3). The Holy Spirit came to the Church as a whole but dwells in individuals. Each member of Christ's Church has the responsibility to keep the fire burning within them. Paul appealed to the Christians in Ephesus not to grieve the Holy Spirit of God (Ephesians 4:30). Being resentful, giving way to outbursts of anger, being overbearingly self-assertive and being abusive will all do that (Ephesians 4:31). Instead Paul says, "Be kind to one another, tender-hearted, forgiving one another, as God in Christ forgave you." (Ephesians 4:32)

Keeping clean

Keeping the fire burning requires that we keep clean.

The Pharisees criticised Jesus for allowing His disciples to eat without washing their hands in a ritually correct way and so their hands were "defiled" (Mark 7:5). But the Lord Jesus explained to His disciples that real uncleanness and defilement are caused by the things that "come out of a person" (Mark 7:20). He went on to list the kind of things that defile: "evil thoughts, vulgar deeds, stealing, murder, unfaithfulness in marriage, greed, meanness, deceit, indecency, envy, insults, pride, and foolishness" (Mark 7:21-22 CEV).

On the positive side James writes, "Religion that is pure and undefiled before God, the Father, is this: to visit orphans and widows in their affliction." (James 1:27)

Providing for leaders

The principle of supporting leaders applies to the Church. When the Lord Jesus sent out the Twelve He told them to preach and perform miracles without taking payment since He had given them the ability to do these things without demanding payment from them (Matthew 10:8). But then He went on to say, "The labourer deserves his food" (Matthew 10:10). There is a distinction between demanding payment and accepting what is offered.

Paul refers to the Lord's words in 1 Corinthians 9:14. In that verse "get their living" has the sense of maintaining life rather than making a fortune. Paul tells Timothy that "elders who rule well", and especially those who preach and teach, should be paid generously (1 Timothy 5:17-18). The emphasis is on the appreciative response of the church rather than on the demands of the preacher.

Separation and Communication

God does not change (Malachi 3:6). He is still holy (John 17:11), completely separate from all that is common or unclean. Is there an "airlock" for us and how does it work?

45

We have been sanctified, made holy "through the offering of the body of Jesus Christ" (Hebrews 10:10). What is even more remarkable is that God intends the Church to be "a holy priesthood", with the purpose of offering "spiritual sacrifices acceptable to God through Jesus Christ" (1 Peter 2:5). So "we have confidence to enter the holy places by the blood of Jesus" (Hebrews 10:19) and we are encouraged to "draw near" (Hebrews 10:22).

In his suffering Job complained that God "is not a man, as I am, that I might answer him, that we should come to trial together. There is no arbiter between us, who might lay his hand on us both" (Job 9:32-33). Our High Priest is both God and man. He knows what it is to be tempted (Hebrews 2.18) and sympathises with our weaknesses (Hebrews 4:15). Paul wrote, "There is one God, and there is one mediator between God and men, the man Christ Jesus"(1Timothy 2:5). He is the answer to Job's prayer.

The Ordination of Priests
Leviticus 8

All the instructions for this ritual had been given to Moses personally (Exodus 28&29). The time had come to go public. It was necessary for the people to know that they had priests and who they were. So Moses was instructed to take Aaron and his sons and the things required for sacrifices and to "assemble all the congregation at the entrance of the tent of meeting" (3).

The rituals took place within the courtyard of the tabernacle. The equipment required for the ceremony of ordination was there. Since the purpose of summoning the people together was that they would be witnesses to the consecration of Aaron and his sons, the people would have to enter the courtyard. The courtyard measured about 50 yards by 25 yards and could not possibly hold every one of the Israelites. So "the congregation" is generally understood to mean here, as it does in other places, the elders, the heads of tribes and families, representing the whole nation. We may picture the elders gathered around the altar of burnt offering, just inside the entrance to the courtyard, able to see all that went on. The events of the day would be reported at home and so everyone would know that Aaron and his sons had been consecrated as priests.

The Calling

The role of High Priest was not something Aaron took upon himself (Hebrews 5:4). He was called to the task by God. While Moses was on Sinai, God told him that Aaron and his sons would serve in the tabernacle (Exodus 27:21).

It was not that Aaron was particularly worthy. Even while Moses was receiving the Law from God, Aaron yielded to the demands of the people to make them an idol and led them in its worship (Exodus 32:1-6). Aaron would have died along with the rest of the people except for Moses' intercession with God (Exodus 32:9-14). What church would have appointed any man with such a record? Yet God persisted in His plan to use Aaron as High Priest for the Israelites and even as a pattern of the Great High Priest who was to come. Amazing grace!

The fact that Aaron did not take the honour upon himself is emphasised by the role that Moses played in the consecration of the priests. Moses brought Aaron and his sons with all the items required to the tent of meeting. Moses assembled the congregation to witness the rituals. Moses washed Aaron and his sons and put the priestly garments on them, both of which the

47

priests would eventually do for themselves (Exodus 30:17-21). In the offering of the sacrifices, Aaron and his sons did what was required of worshippers, for instance in placing their hands on the heads of the animals (14, 18, 22), while it was Moses who performed the tasks of a priest in dealing with the blood and the various parts of the animals.

Moses set the whole tone of the day by saying at the start, "This is the thing that the LORD has commanded to be done" (5).The matter is put beyond doubt by the statement that Moses was doing what the LORD had commanded him, a statement which is made at every stage of the proceedings (9,13,17,21,29,34,35,36).

It was God who called and consecrated Aaron and his sons. Moses was acting as God's agent.

The Washing

Whenever a priest went on duty he was to wash his hands and his feet using the water in the bronze basin (Exodus 30:18-21). The washing was symbolic of mental and spiritual cleanliness.

Before Moses died he reminded the Israelites of God's laws and explained how to apply them when they were settled in the Promised Land. In particular, he instructed them that if murder was committed by an unknown assailant, the elders of the town, in a special ceremony involving sacrifice, were to wash their hands and say, "Our hands did not shed this blood, nor did our eyes see it shed" (Deuteronomy 21:1-9). In a similar way the priest was being challenged to state in symbol and in God's presence that he was not secretly and unrepentantly clinging on to sin.

David asked who could stand in God's holy place. His answer was that it had to be one who had clean hands and was pure in heart and soul (Psalm 24:3-4).

The Clothing

All priests, Aaron and his sons, were to wear linen undergarments covering hips and thighs (Exodus 28:42). They each wore a linen coat closed by a linen sash which was embroidered. Aaron wore a linen turban and his sons wore linen caps (Exodus 28:39-40).

Because they were on holy ground, they were all barefoot (Exodus 3:5; Joshua 5:15).

There were four items which were for the exclusive use of the High Priest. These were the robe, the ephod and the breast-piece (Exodus 28:4), and the gold plate which was fastened to the turban (Exodus 28:36-38).

The robe reached below the knees. It was woven in one piece of blue cloth without a seam with a hole for the head. Attached to the hem were a number of gold bells. Between the bells were pomegranates made from blue,

48

purple and scarlet yarns (Exodus 28:31-35). The pomegranates would strike the bells, causing them to ring softly as the priest went about his work.

The ephod was like a tabard made "of gold, of blue and purple and scarlet yarns, and of fine twined linen" (Exodus 28:6). Two onyx stones, secured with gold filigree, were set, one on each of the shoulder-pieces of the ephod. Each stone was engraved with six of the names of the tribes of Israel (Exodus 28:9-10). Aaron was to bear these names "before the LORD on his two shoulders for remembrance" (Exodus 28:12).

The breast-piece was made of the same materials as the ephod and attached to it (Exodus 28:15-30). Set in the breast-piece were twelve precious stones in four rows. On each stone was engraved one of the names of the twelve tribes. In the pocket formed by the breast-piece were the Urim and Thummim (Exodus 28:30) which were probably used like simple dice to determine God's will. The breast-piece is described as "a breast-piece of judgment" (Exodus 28:15). The significance of this item seems to be that, in wearing it in the Holy Place, "before the LORD", Aaron would be seeking to know God's will for the nation.

Attached to the turban was a gold plate described by some as a tiara and by others as a diadem. It was inscribed with the words "HOLY TO THE LORD". It would remind the wearer that Israel was set apart for God's exclusive service and that the priest entered the Holy Place only after the sin of the nation had been dealt with (Exodus 28:36-38).

The garments are described in Exodus 28 in great detail. For most of the details, any symbolic significance is not explained. However, two things are clear.

The first is that the gold, blue, purple, scarlet and fine linen used to make the garments are the same materials and colours used to make the tabernacle, in particular the screen that was across the entrance to the tent (Exodus 26:36-37). The garments belonged exclusively to the tabernacle. They were the robes of office for those who ministered there.

The second is that God had told Moses that the garments were to be "for glory and for beauty" (Exodus 28:2&40). God's purpose was to transform ordinary men into holy priests and to inspire respect and reverence for the priestly office in the hearts and minds of the congregation.

Seeing Aaron dressed so splendidly the congregation may have thought that he was ready to start work, that now they had a High Priest. But there was much to be done still.

The Anointing

Aaron and his sons were all to be anointed (Exodus 30:30). But a distinction is made in Leviticus 8 between the High Priest and the priests.

Aaron was anointed by having anointing oil poured on his head (12) even before his sons had their priestly garments put on (13). It was not until after the sin offering and the burnt offering had been made that the sons were anointed, and then they and Aaron were anointed with the blood of the ram of ordination (22-24). Finally, after all the sacrifices had been made, Aaron and his garments and his sons and their garments were anointed. This was done, not by pouring oil on their heads, but by sprinkling them and their garments with a mixture of oil and of blood from the altar (30).

It is worth noting that the same oil had been used to anoint the tabernacle and all that was in it, the altar and all its utensils and the basin and its stand (10-11). The blood had been applied to the horns of the altar, poured at its base or thrown against its sides (15, 19, 24). So their consecration as priests was closely bound together with the tabernacle and its furniture. They had no right to pull rank in the community or to lord it over others simply because they were priests. Their status and function as priests was all to do with the purpose and function of the tabernacle.

The purpose of the anointing was "to consecrate" them (12&30), that is, to set them apart for the service of God. They were anointed with blood on their right ears, the thumbs of their right hands and on the big toes of their right feet (23-24). It was a case of the part representing the whole and of the right side being the most important (cf. Genesis 48:17). Every part of them and every action was set apart for God.

To serve God requires supernatural enabling. When David was anointed with oil to be king "the Spirit of the LORD rushed upon David from that day forward" (1 Samuel 16:13). David was able to calm Saul's spirit with his music, to kill a lion and a bear and to defeat Goliath. So Aaron and his sons were given God's enabling to serve him. They did not always depend upon that enabling, and as a result made mistakes (Leviticus 10:1-2; Numbers 12).

The Offerings

Being washed, clothed in wonderful robes and anointed was not enough. Blood sacrifice was necessary if they were to be acceptable and fit to serve God. The sin offering followed the procedure of Leviticus 4:3-12, except that no blood was applied within the sanctuary since, as yet, no priest had entered the Holy Place. The burnt offering was made according to the instructions in Leviticus 1.

The ram of ordination was sacrificed according to the pattern of a peace offering given in chapter 3. However, it was evidently meant to be looked upon as special: a ram was specified, it was referred to as "the ram of ordination", and its blood was used to anoint Aaron and his sons. Furthermore, whereas in the peace offering the breast and thigh were given to the priest (7:31-32), the

50

breast of the ram of ordination was given to Moses (29) but the thigh was given to God, burnt on the altar (26-28). Once again it is shown that Aaron is being consecrated by God with Moses acting as priest on God's behalf.

With each offering Moses played the part of priest. Aaron and his sons were the worshippers. They would eventually function as priests but, at that time, they were the ones who needed forgiveness and atonement, they needed to be consecrated and ordained.

The Waiting

Following that day of ordination, Aaron and his sons were to stay within the courtyard of the tabernacle for a week (33). God's command to Moses had been, "Through seven days you shall ordain them." On each day Moses was to offer a bull as a sin offering (Exodus 29:35, 36).

The Hebrew words translated "ordain" and "ordination" (22, 28, 29, 31, 33) convey the idea of filling. It could be used of the setting for a precious stone. Without the gem it was empty. It needed filling to perform its function. It would take a week to ordain Aaron and his sons (33) so that, cleansed and filled, they could function as priests.

The Great High Priest

Moses was a prophet who also, at least for a time, fulfilled the role of priest. God promised that He would raise up a prophet like Moses (Deuteronomy 18:15-18). That Jesus thought of Himself as a prophet is implied in Luke 13:33. Both Peter and Stephen spoke of Jesus as fulfilling God's promise to Moses (Acts 3:22-26; 7:37). Just as Moses, acting on God's behalf, ordained Aaron, so Jesus chose and appointed others to His service (John 15:16). As Aaron was called and ordained by God, "So also Christ did not exalt Himself to be made a high priest, but was appointed by Him who said to Him, 'You are my Son, today I have begotten you'" (Hebrews 5:4-5).

Jesus did not need to be washed. He never sinned in deed or in word (1 Peter 2:22). He chose to submit to the symbolic washing of baptism in order to identify with repentant sinners (Matthew 3:13-15). Neither did He need to have sacrifices offered for His forgiveness and atonement. The sacrifice He made was the sacrifice of Himself for the sins of others (Hebrews 7:26-27).

It was foretold that there would be nothing in the physical appearance of God's Servant which people would find attractive (Isaiah 53:2-3). Jesus wore an undergarment which was woven without a seam (John 19:23). According to Josephus, the robe of the high priest was woven in that way. But it was, apparently, a common way of weaving in New Testament times and would not have been seen as special. Certainly, as a result of crucifixion, His appearance was "marred beyond human semblance" (Isaiah 52:14). But, for those with eyes to see, He displayed the glory of "the only Son from the

Father, full of grace and truth" (John 1:14). Now risen and exalted, He is clothed in robes of glory and beauty (Revelation 1:12-16).

Aaron's ordination took a week. For Jesus also there were periods of preparation. Although as a twelve-year-old He had an understanding of spiritual matters which amazed the religious leaders, and although He knew that He had a special relationship with God (Luke 2:42-49), He waited until He was thirty before beginning His ministry (Luke 3:23). This was the age at which Levites began their service (Numbers 4:3) and at which a man was considered to be fully mature. Waiting was part of the process by which Jesus became "like His brothers in every respect" (Hebrews 2:17). He was tempted in every respect as we are, yet without sin (Hebrews 4:15). In these ways He was perfectly prepared to be our High Priest, our Representative and our Substitute. At Jesus' baptism, He was anointed by the Spirit and received the Father's public seal of approval (Matthew 3:16-17). It would have seemed that He was ready to begin His ministry. But He was led by the Spirit into the wilderness (Matthew 4:1-11) and there, resisting all the devil's temptations, He determined what sort of Messiah He was to be.

The Christian's "Ordination"

Paul addresses the Christians in Colossae as "God's chosen ones" (Colossians 3:12). Those God chooses He also calls. He calls us "to belong to Jesus Christ" (Romans 1:6), to live for Him and for Him alone. Similarly we are "called to be saints" (1 Corinthians 1:2), to be set apart for Him and for Him alone. In all of this it is clear that as with Aaron, so with the Christian, God takes the initiative.

As it was for Aaron, so there is a symbolic washing for those who would follow Christ. John's baptism was a baptism of repentance, a symbolic washing away and abandonment of old *deeds*, and an appeal for forgiveness (Acts 19:1-6). Christian baptism is more than that. It is a symbolic washing away and putting to death of an old *life*, and a rising to a new one (Romans 6:1-4). The real washing of believers is a matter of the mind and the spirit. It is effected through the blood of Jesus (1 John 1:7), the word of the Gospel (Ephesians 5:26; cf. John 15:3), and by the work of the Holy Spirit (Titus 3:5).

A Christian is to be suitably clothed. Deeds that may be pleasing to us but are unacceptable to God are likened to a filthy garment (Isaiah 64:6). Because God has chosen us, because He has set us apart for Himself, and because He loves us, we should put on the garments of "compassion, kindness, humility, meekness, and patience, bearing with one another and forgiving each another." (Colossians 3:12-13)

It takes time to prepare a Christian for God's service. Jesus' disciples spent three years with Him listening to His teaching and occasionally being sent out to preach and heal (Matthew 10:1ff). But the primary purpose was that they should "be with Him" (Mark 3:14), learning from Him through His personal influence in their lives. After the Resurrection they had to wait in Jerusalem for forty days (Acts 1). They were not idle, but Jesus continued to teach them. No doubt their understanding was growing in the light of the Cross and the Resurrection, but it was still faulty (Acts 1:6). They had to wait for the coming of the Holy Spirit who would teach them all they needed to know and remind them of all that Jesus had said (John 14:26).

It takes time to prepare a Christian for God's service. There is a first rung on every ladder and each rung has to be taken a step at a time. We do not go to the top in one stride as many young, enthusiastic Christians would like. God prepares us for one task and, as we do that in His strength, He is preparing us for the next. He uses our successes and He uses our failures. All the time the most important thing is not what we are doing for Him but what He is doing for us, that is, using everything to make us like his Son (Romans 8:28-29).

used to mean a shout of joy (Psalm 20:5) and they had plenty to rejoice about. The fire consumed in a moment the carcasses smouldering on the altar. This showed them that the sacrifices were accepted completely, that cleansing and atonement were complete. The glimpse of glory and the fire proved that God really was living among them. They need fear no foe and they would not lack any necessity. They fell on their faces in worship.

Things could not get better but, because of the human factor, things could get worse and they did.

The Human Factor

Why was it wrong for Nadab and Abihu to offer incense, so seriously wrong that they died for it? Several suggestions have been made but none is conclusive. The only clear statements are that it was "unauthorised" and that it was something which God "had not commanded them" (10:1). They should have known from all that Moses had said during the eight days of ordination that the most important thing about every sacrifice and every ritual was that it was what God had commanded to be done (e.g. 9:6).

What possessed them to follow their own wishes in this way? When God spoke to Aaron it was to command that priests must not drink alcohol before going on duty (10:8-11). This seems a strange matter to talk about in the circumstances, but perhaps in the celebrations following the appearance of God the two men had drunk too much and had been "led astray" (Proverbs 20:1). God then went on to give Aaron the instructions about distinguishing "between the holy and the common, and between the unclean and the clean". Perhaps under the influence of alcohol Nadab and Abihu had failed to "distinguish between the holy and the common", and so forgot that what mattered was not what they wanted to do but what God had commanded should be done. They "got carried away". Their ability to make sound judgment had been ruined (Isaiah 28:7).

Serious Sin, Severe Punishment

The punishment seems very severe. But, through Moses, God immediately explains why (10:3). If God had not acted it would have raised questions about His own purity, alertness and power. Priests are in a very special position in relation to God and the eyes of the people are on them. Not only must they teach the people to distinguish between holy and common but they must practise what they preach. This was the beginning of the priesthood and God was putting His stamp of approval on Aaron and his sons. Drunken disobedience could not be included lest it set a pattern for the future. Eventually priests were to be judges in criminal and civil matters and the people were to adhere to their decisions (Deuteronomy 17:9-13) so their judgments must not be distorted through intoxication.

56

Aaron's Priesthood Confirmed

Aaron must have found the death of his sons hard to bear especially since he was not allowed to join in the customary mourning for them. He must not appear to either condone his sons' behaviour or to find fault with God. The bodies were carried away by Aaron's nephews (10:4-5) while he and his sons remained within the courtyard (10:6-7).

There was encouragement for Aaron. He may have blamed himself, as fathers tend to do, for his sons' behaviour. He may have wondered if, because of that, he too would be disqualified. But God spoke to Aaron about the future (10:8-11), and did so directly without going through Moses. And Moses instructed Aaron to continue with the rituals which had been interrupted by the death of his sons (10:12-15). The sacrifices would be complete only when the grain offering and the breast and thigh from the peace offerings had been eaten as instructed. So Aaron and his sons are confirmed in their roles.

A Difference of Opinion

The goat of the sin offering should have been eaten too but Aaron and his sons burned it (10:16). Moses was angry because the ritual had not been carried out as directed. Aaron's reply (10:19) may mean that in offering the incense his sons had entered the holy place and so that had been defiled. So, although the blood of the sin offering had not been sprinkled before the curtain (4:5-7), Aaron thought that it would be wrong to eat the meat and that it should be burned (4:8-12). When Moses heard Aaron's explanation he approved (10:20). There are circumstances in which none of the rules seem to apply, but a sincere desire to please God is enough.

The Glory Departs

The glory of God remained with them throughout their wanderings (Exodus 40:38; Numbers 14:10; 16:19; 16:42; 20:6).

The next possible reference to God's glory is in 1 Samuel 4:22 when the daughter-in-law of Eli the high priest named her son Ichabod saying, "The glory has departed from Israel, for the ark of God has been captured." Whatever she meant by "the glory", the glory of God had departed long before. This is evidenced by the behaviour of Eli's sons (1 Samuel 2:12-22), by the fact that "the word of the LORD was rare in those days; there was no frequent vision" (1 Samuel 3:1), and by the way the people treated the ark like a talisman (1 Samuel 4:3).

The glory of God came again when the ark was brought into Solomon's new temple (1 Kings 8:11). But as the years went by the nation steadily moved further from God's ways until God allowed their enemies to overwhelm them and they were taken into exile. As noted in a previous chapter, the reason for this was explained through Ezekiel in a vision; the glory of God had left the temple (Ezekiel 10:18) and Jerusalem (Ezekiel 10:19).

The Glory Promised

Even as God's people were showing that they were not fit to have God dwelling among them, God promised that the time would come when the whole world would see His glory (Numbers 14:21; Isaiah 40:5).

When the Word, God the Son, became a man He "pitched his tent" among us so that the glory of God was seen in Him. It was seen in His life of grace and truth (John 1:14). Grace was seen in bringing God's free salvation to the world (John 3:16-17). To do that He must go to the Cross, and it is there, most remarkably, that the glory of God, totally unlike any glory of man, is seen (John 12:23); God giving His Son to die for those who had made themselves his enemies (Romans 5:8). Truth was seen in everything He said and did; He was the very embodiment of truth (John 14:6).

The glory of God displayed in Jesus of Nazareth was not recognised by the rulers of His day and they "crucified the Lord of glory" (1 Corinthians 2:8). But His glory will be seen at His return (Titus 2:13) and everyone will see Him (Revelation 1:7). Through Christ's perfect sacrifice of Himself God is present in the Church. In the New Jerusalem, the glorified Church, "the glory of God gives it light, and its lamp is the Lamb" (Revelation 21.23). There will be no "Nadab and Abihu incidents" there, no consuming fire of judgment, since the distinction between holy and unclean will be perfect and "nothing unclean will ever enter it" (Revelation 21:27). There will be no death or mourning there (Revelation 21:3-4).

Meanwhile

Until "the day dawns and the shadows flee away", God's Word is our lamp and light (Psalm 119:105). God's Word must be properly understood, so, like the priests (10.11), church leaders must be able to teach (1 Timothy 3:2) and their judgment must not be clouded by alcohol (1 Timothy 3:3). As with the priests, much has been given teachers (Ephesians 4:8-12) so much is required of them (Luke 12:48) and they will be judged with greater strictness (James 3:1).

The distinction between what God regards as holy and what He sees as unclean must be taught. Aaron and his sons had to learn that no matter how good their intentions they were no substitute for exact obedience. Ananias and Sapphira may have thought that a demonstration of generosity was good enough. But their attempt at deception was an offence against God. The belief that God could be deceived could not be allowed to go unchecked, especially at the beginning of the Church, and they were punished with great severity (Acts 5:1-11).

58

Teachers need to give Biblical guidance in matters of priorities. Aaron had to put the service of God first, even before the concerns of family (10:6-7). When a disciple asked Jesus to wait for him while he attended his father's funeral, Jesus' reply was, "Follow me, and let the dead bury their own dead" (Matthew 8:21-22). When family matters conflict, not merely with what other Christians expect of us, but with what God's Word requires, then following Christ must come first.

Bible teachers do not always agree on details. Initially Moses and Aaron did not see eye to eye over what should be done with the meat from the goat of the sin offering. Both men wanted to do what was God-pleasing and Moses had the grace to accept that Aaron had good reason for believing that what he did was right and for acting in accordance with that belief. As the apostle Paul wrote, "One person believes he may eat anything, while the weak person eats only vegetables" (Romans 14:2) and, "One person esteems one day as better than another, while another esteems all days alike" (Romans 14:5). The guiding principles are that we will each have to give an account of ourselves, not to other Christians but to God (Romans 14:12), and that we should make it our aim to neither pass judgment on another Christian, nor to hinder them in their aim to live for Christ (Romans 14:13). The aim of teachers should be, not to become great theologians so as to be able to win all the arguments, but to be able to lead God's people to live Christ-like lives and to live Christ-like lives themselves.

Jesus' prayer for those who believe in Him was that they would see His glory (John 17:24). For Nadab and Abihu God's glory was there but, through disobedience, they were expelled from it forever. That illustrates the situation for every human being. All have disobeyed God and have fallen short of His glory (Romans 3:23). But in His prayer Jesus not only prayed that believers would see His glory, but also said that He had given it to them (John 17:22). And Paul assures the Christians of Rome that God's purpose for those He has called is that they should be like His Son (Romans 8:29) and goes on to say that God has "glorified" them (Romans 8:30). So the glory that Jesus gives is Christ-likeness. As far as God is concerned the work is done and He has lifted us up to glory, to sit with Christ in the heavenly places (Ephesians 2:6). But from our point of view it is the work of a lifetime. As by the Spirit within we see God's glory, we begin to reflect it as Moses did (Exodus 34:29), and so, "from one degree of glory to another" God is changing us by His Spirit to make us like His Son (2 Corinthians 3:7-18).

Holy Eating
Leviticus 11

Aaron had been confirmed in his role as High Priest. Moses had insisted that Aaron complete the sacrificial rituals of his ordination (10:12-15); God had told him that his tasks in the future would include maintaining the distinction "between the holy and the common, and between the unclean and the clean" and teaching the people all God's Law given through Moses (10:10-11). God had not yet explained how to distinguish between holy and common, clean and unclean but in chapters 11 to 15 He does so. In chapter 11 God explains what is required in the way of holy eating (46-47).

In reading this chapter one has to bear in mind that it is reckoned that only forty percent of the creatures named here can be identified with accuracy.

Animals

The way the Israelites had to distinguish between clean and unclean animals was very simple. Those who had cloven hooves and chewed the cud were clean and could be eaten. Those who met only one of those requirements or none were unclean and must not be eaten. Four unclean animals are named, the camel, the rock-badger, the hare and the pig.

The camel does in fact satisfy the rules but is listed as unclean. This may be because it has such a thick sole that the cloven hooves are not obvious. A camel may be touched while alive and used for transport, and, by doing so, a person would not become unclean. But its meat must not be eaten, its carcass is unclean (8), and anyone who touches its carcass becomes unclean (26).

When a clean animal dies of natural causes it becomes unclean (39-40). Eating its flesh or touching its carcass renders the person unclean.

Water Creatures

The rule for these was simple. Anything with both fins and scales could be eaten (9). Other creatures, such as shellfish and crabs, must not be eaten and their carcasses must be avoided (10-11).

Birds

No simple rule was given for birds but a list was given of those which must not be eaten (13-19). Bearing in mind the difficulty of accurate identification, it seems that the list is of birds which are predators or eaters of carrion.

Insects

Insects were to be separated into clean and unclean by the way they move when on the ground. Those that crawl (20 & 23) were unclean. Those that hop, using two legs as birds do, the locust, cricket and grasshopper, could be eaten (21 & 22).

Swarming Creatures

Swarming creatures are those which move along the ground by crawling or wriggling. There is also the idea of existing together in great numbers. All swarming creatures are unclean (41). A list is given (29-30). This is expanded later (41-43) in a way that would include, among other things, worms and snakes.

Swarming creatures would very often have found their way into houses. So what rules apply, especially when such a creature is found dead?

The person who had to deal with the carcass would become unclean and remain so for the rest of the day (31). The article on which the carcass was found became unclean. If it was of wood, or a garment, a skin or a sack, it had to be soaked in water and remain there for the rest of the day. At the end of that time it would be clean (32). An earthenware vessel must be broken (33). Anything in such a vessel that was intended for eating or drinking would be unclean (34). A contaminated oven or stove must never be used again; it must be smashed (35). Springs and cisterns were exempt (36) as was seed intended for sowing (37). Seed in preparation for cooking would be unclean (38).

Dealing with Uncleanness

When anything unclean was touched, whether out of necessity or by accident, the solution God required was to wash one's clothes and remain unclean for the rest of the day (25, 28, 40). Being unclean would have meant isolating oneself from others and excluding oneself from the tabernacle and its rituals. So fellowship with God and God's people was put on hold. If anyone failed to do this they would be guilty before God. If at a later date they realised that they had become unclean but had failed to deal with their uncleanness in the required way, they were required to offer a sin offering (5:2ff). In that way atonement was made (5:6) and fellowship was restored.

The Reason for the Rules

It cannot be that those creatures declared unclean are inherently evil. At creation God declared all living creatures "good" (Genesis 1:21, 25); God commanded the ravens (15) to feed Elijah (1 Kings 17:2-6); God used "the face of an eagle" (13) when revealing something of his likeness to Ezekiel (Ezekiel 1:10); and the Lord Jesus "declared all foods clean" (Mark 7:19).

Various suggestions have been made to explain the logic behind these prohibitions. One is that they were given for reasons of hygiene. Pigs and hares, for example, carry diseases and God would want to protect His people from them. But pagans who ate pigs and hares dealt with the risk of infection by careful cooking. The Israelites must have known how to cook properly since some of the animals that are designated clean also carried diseases.

61

Another way of explaining the significance of the rules is to treat them as allegories. An example of this approach is to say that the chewing of the cud is a reminder to meditate on the law; on the other hand Israelites ought not to be like pigs by wallowing in the mud of sin or be timid like hares. There are difficulties with this kind of approach. The explanations are down to one's imagination, so the number of explanations is limitless. There is no way of knowing how valid an explanation is and this is complicated by the lack of certainty about the identity of many of these creatures.

The pig was used in pagan rituals, so perhaps the purpose of the rules was to distinguish Israelite rituals from that of pagans. But the bull, included among the clean and required in some sacrifices, was the common symbol of the fertility cults.

Because of the difficulties involved in finding a convincing explanation, it has been suggested that the right approach is to say that only God knows the reason for His rules and it is a matter of obeying simply because it is what God has commanded. This is certainly a valid reason for obedience whether or not an explanation is given.

God's Reason

In fact God does give a reason for the rules. He said, "I am the LORD who brought you up out of the land of Egypt to be your God. You shall therefore be holy, for I am holy" (45). The laws of Leviticus called for rituals which symbolised spiritual truths. The dietary laws required behaviour which symbolised the holiness that God required of His people.

God made man in His image (Genesis 1:27). In God's eyes the normal condition for humans is to be like Him, that is, to be holy. To be holy is to be normal in the way God intended.

This is demonstrated in Leviticus. Priests had to allow their hair and beards to grow without any interference, that is, to grow normally (21:5); in that way, God said, "They shall be holy" (21:60). For a descendant of Aaron to qualify for the priesthood he had to be without abnormality or defect (21:17-23), otherwise the sanctuary would be profaned.

So creatures that did not conform to the rules of what was understood to be normal for a particular category or did not fit into any category, creatures that were "neither fish nor flesh nor fowl", were abnormal and therefore unclean.

The animals that God pronounced as clean and therefore edible were those which would be seen as normal by the Israelites. Being keepers of flocks and herds, they were familiar with those that were cloven-hoofed and cud-chewing and they would consider these characteristics as normal. The birds which were to be considered unclean were the predators and eaters of carrion. They ate blood and fed on the dead, both of which were forbidden to the Israelites so were not normal. They were birds which had to do with death, and death is the condition which is as far from God's norm as it is possible to be. Clean insects were those which, when on the ground, move in a way which is normal for creatures of the air, using two legs to hop as birds do. Normally fish have fins and scales. Creatures that swarm do not conform to any norm and so were to be considered unclean.

A Diet for God's People

To conform to the dietary rules symbolised holiness. So holiness was not a matter just for the tabernacle and the sacrifices but a matter for everyday life. Every meal would be a reminder that the LORD was their God, they were His people and He called them to be holy (45). Observing the rules did not make them God's people any more than offering the sacrifices did. They were to observe the rules because they were God's people.

Creation

The dietary laws are symbolic not literal. It does not follow from them that human beings should regard "unclean" creatures as disgusting or unnecessary. After six days of creation, in God's eyes, "everything" was "very good" (Genesis 1:31). God claims ownership of every living thing (Psalm 50:10-11). In his rebuke of Job, God refers to two birds, the hawk and the eagle, listed as unclean in Leviticus 11, and infers that their wonderful flying ability comes through God's command and control (Job 39:26-27). The rock badger and the lizard, to be regarded as unclean for eating purposes by the Israelites, are referred to as "exceedingly wise" (Proverbs 30:24-28). So every living thing is part of God's good creation, is to be treated with respect and may even teach lessons by its way of life.

Jews and Gentiles

By New Testament times, the Jews had come to look upon observing the dietary laws as equating to holiness. The fact that they were symbolic had been forgotten. A Jew, it was thought, was made holy by observing these laws, and by doing so, was made acceptable to God. As time went by the rabbis had added to the laws of Leviticus 11 by saying that hands must be washed before eating in case there was something unclean on the hands which would defile the eater. So in this case, as with many of the Old Testament laws, the burden of obedience was made heavier and became almost unbearable (Luke 11:46). For the religious leaders it was obvious heresy for Jesus to say that what a person eats does not defile him. He said that it is the evil that comes out that defiles because it has its origins in the heart. In this way, as Mark points out, Jesus "declared all foods clean" (Mark 7:18-23).

The result of the strict rabbinical interpretation of the dietary laws was that Jews would not eat with a Gentile nor even enter a Gentile house (Acts 11:3). This attitude resulted in the first Christians (who were Jews) tending to preach the Gospel only to Jews (Acts 11:19). Two things happened to correct this.

Peter was given a vision in which he was shown "unclean" animals and told to eat of them. When he refused he was told, "What God has made clean, do not call common" (Acts 10:15). Subsequently, Peter, in obedience to the message of the vision and the prompting of the Holy Spirit, went to Caesarea and preached the Gospel to Cornelius and his relatives and friends, all of whom were Gentiles (Acts 10:24-43). Everyone who heard the Gospel believed, received the Holy Spirit and was baptized (Acts 10:44-48).

At about the same time, Christian Jews from Cyprus and Cyrene went to Antioch and preached the Gospel to Gentiles there. A great number of them believed. Barnabas was sent to Antioch. When he saw what God was doing there he fetched Paul from Tarsus and together they taught the new Gentile Christians (Acts 11:20-26).

The whole question of the relevance to Christians, not only of the dietary laws, but of all the ritual laws of the Old Testament, had to be resolved. The debate and decision are recorded in Acts 15. Paul and Barnabas related what had been going on in Antioch, and Peter told of his experiences in Caesarea. It was recognized that what was happening had been foretold (Amos 9:11-12; Acts 15:15-18), and it was resolved that the only requirements of Gentile Christians should be that they "abstain from the things polluted by idols, and from sexual immorality, and from what has been strangled, and from blood" (Acts 15:20). The reason they insisted on the prohibition about blood may have been because it goes back to the time of Noah (Genesis 9:4), pre-dates the laws of Leviticus and would be understood to apply to the whole human race. The list of requirements was something of a compromise but it opened the way for the preaching of the Gospel to Gentiles without reference to Jewish rituals.

So it came about that Gentiles, "having no hope and without God in the world", who were far away from God, have been, "in Christ Jesus", "brought near by the blood of Christ" (Ephesians 2:11-13). Christ gave Himself to abolish the ritual law which divided Jew from Gentile (Ephesians 2:14-15). Now there is "neither Jew nor Greek ... for you are all one in Christ Jesus" (Galatians 3:28).

Be Holy

Although the food laws have been made redundant through the death of Christ and, in Christ, they no longer separate Gentile from Jew, there remains a need for God's people to live in a way that distinguishes them from those who are not His. Peter appeals to his readers to be holy in all their conduct and appeals to Leviticus 11:44 as his authority for doing so (1 Peter 1:16). It is God's purpose that every Christian should be holy in reality (Colossians 1:22), rather than merely in symbolic ritual. It will be readily understood that holiness requires obeying God's moral laws, summarised in the Ten Commandments, and even more concisely in the two great commandments to love God and to love one's neighbour as oneself (Matthew 22:36-40). But it also requires a degree of separation from those who are not God's people.

Keep Separate

When Daniel was taken to Babylon he had to decide to what extent he would conform to the foreign culture. He submitted to the education in language and literature (Daniel 1:4-5) but he refused the rich food from the king's table (Daniel 1:8). This was not simply a matter of obeying the rules of Leviticus 11. For one thing it specifically states that he refused the king's wine, and there is no mention of wine in the dietary laws. For another, all food in Babylon would have been "unclean" (Ezekiel 4:13). It was the king's food and wine in particular that Daniel was refusing. To share a meal with someone was to commit to fellowship as in the peace offering of Leviticus 3. Daniel had to keep himself free of such a commitment. The days would come when Daniel would have to speak God's message to Nebuchadnezzar without being under any obligation to give the king what he wanted or to tell him what he wanted to hear.

Paul appealed to the Christians in Corinth not to be "unequally yoked with unbelievers". The picture is of two mismatched animals being yoked together. One of them is obliged to go along with the other unless he breaks the yoke. Paul expands the idea in the following verses by using words like partnership, fellowship, accord and agreement. He emphasises the impracticality of mismatched unions by getting the Corinthians to imagine righteousness and lawlessness, or light and darkness working together, or Christ co-operating with Satan. These relationships are impossible (2 Corinthians 6:14-16). In verses 16 to 18, Paul shows that the principles governing the behaviour of God's people remain unchanged by referring to Old Testament passages, one of them being in Leviticus 26.

Paul was not writing about being simply friends or acquaintances, but about relationships which require the partners to go along together in all that is done. The Lord Jesus, in His prayer, did not ask that His disciples should be taken out of the world. In fact He said that He was sending them into the world. But He said that they were "not of the world" and asked that they would be kept "from the evil one" (John 17:15-18). Christians need to know how unbelievers think, what is important to them, what their topics of conversation are. We need to do as Ezekiel did, that is to "sit where they are dwelling" (Ezekiel 3:15). Otherwise it will be impossible to communicate the Gospel to them in a way to which they can relate. But we must be wary of slipping into the world's ways of thinking and behaving.

Diet Matters

Our diet has no effect on our relationship with God. As the apostle wrote, "Food will not commend us to God" (1 Corinthians 8:8). Whether we eat or not makes no difference. It is by the death of God's Son that we have been reconciled to Him (Romans 5:10). But what a Christian eats and drinks does matter for two reasons.

One is that my behaviour may influence another believer for good or ill.

In New Testament times, much of the meat for sale was from animals offered in sacrifice to pagan gods. Was it right for a Christian to eat meat with such heathen associations, especially when eating it might be seen as taking part in a pagan fellowship meal? The Christians in Corinth evidently asked Paul about this (1 Corinthians 8 to 10). Paul replied that, on the one hand, idols have "no real existence" so meat offered to them had not been really affected in any way. But, on the other hand, some Christians had not yet shaken off their pagan past and may have still believed that pagan gods were real. They, on seeing another believer eating meat that had been offered to an idol, could have thought that believer was engaged in idol worship and have been drawn into idol worship themselves. Paul's conclusion is, "If food makes my brother stumble, I will never eat meat, lest I make my brother stumble" (1 Corinthians 8:13).

Alcohol is close to a modern day equivalent. It may be argued that, in moderation it does no harm. However, my example could lead another Christian into excessive drinking. To the church in Rome Paul wrote, "It is good not to eat meat or drink wine or do anything that causes your brother to stumble" (Romans 14:21).

The other reason that diet matters is that a Christian's body is God's property and has become a dwelling place of God by the Spirit (1 Corinthians 6:19-20). As Christians we ought to be careful how we treat what belongs to God. Whatever a Christian does should glorify God (1 Corinthians 10:31), and that includes eating and drinking.

66

Bodily Purity and Discharges
Leviticus 12 and 15

Leviticus 12 deals with the rituals God required after a woman had given birth. Chapters 13 and 14 deal with the problems of skin diseases, then chapter 15 returns to the reproductive process in so far as emissions from sexual organs are concerned. In 12:2&5 there is a reference to the instructions of 15:19-24. This seems to indicate that God gave the rules concerning women's menstruation before those of giving birth. So it seems sensible to think about chapters 12 and 15 together.

Ceremonial not Moral Impurity

The uncleanness God speaks about in these chapters is ceremonial not moral. The Scriptures make it clear that there is nothing sinful about licit sexual intercourse or its result in giving birth. At creation God's command to men and women was, "Be fruitful and multiply" (Genesis 1:28). Childlessness was to be God's judgement on illicit sex (Leviticus 20:20), while children were to be regarded as a blessing from God (Psalm 127:3-5). The Song of Solomon celebrates the sexual relationship between husband and wife. On the other hand, "the LORD put Onan to death" because he deliberately failed to complete the sexual act with his dead brother's wife (Genesis 38:8-10). He disobeyed God's law which is spelt out in Deuteronomy 25:5-10, that he should produce offspring by his childless sister-in-law so that his brother's name and line should not die out. Sexual intercourse was commanded. Childbirth was intended. There is nothing sinful about licit sexual intercourse or its result in giving birth.

Matters of Life or Death

The cause of the uncleanness following childbirth is made clear in 12:7. We read there that, when the procedures for the mother's purifying have been completed, "Then she shall be clean from the flow of her blood." It is not the giving birth but her post-natal discharge that makes her ceremonially unclean.

God said that "the life of the flesh is in the blood" and that he had given it for his people on the altar to make atonement (17:11). Blood given at the altar had an unlimited power to cleanse from defilement; blood in the right place brings great blessing. But blood in meat for human consumption must be removed or it would result in death (17:3-14); blood in the wrong place is serious. Loss of blood represented loss of life, and the seriousness of this was to be acknowledged through the purification process that was to follow childbirth.

A similar acknowledgement was to be made in the purification processes following menstruation (15:19-24), or more prolonged vaginal discharges (15:25-30).

Discharges from the male genitals also have to do with life and death. Whether it is a disease that interferes with the normal reproductive process (15:2-15), or a discharge of semen outside a woman's body (15:16-17), both have to do with a failure to bring life.

The rule about normal sexual intercourse between man and wife (18) was simply a matter of acknowledging that it belonged to the realm of the "common" rather than to the "holy" (compare Exodus 19:15).

Contagion

Uncleanness was serious because it was contagious. The uncleanness could be passed to things which the unclean person touched (15:4, 12, 20, 26). It could also be passed on to other people. This could happen simply by touching or being touched by the person who was unclean (15:7, 10, 19, 27), by being spat on (15:8), or by coming into contact with anything on which they had sat or lain (15:5, 6, 10, 21, 22, 27).

If a man and a woman were engaged in sexual intercourse when her period began, then the man became subject to the same conditions as the woman (15:24).

Following childbirth, a woman's uncleanness would be as contagious as during menstruation for seven days after the birth of a son (12:2) and for two weeks after the birth of a daughter (12:5).

Most seriously, uncleanness would defile God's sanctuary. So remaining unclean for a set period of time meant, not only keeping away from other people, but also staying away from the Tabernacle and its holy rituals (12:4). This would mean, for example, not being allowed to attend the feast which would follow a peace offering (7:20). Defiling God's dwelling place would result in death, so the people had to be separated from their uncleanness (15:31).

Purification Processes

Separation from uncleanness was achieved by observing prescribed purification processes.

Secondary uncleanness was dealt with by washing and by remaining unclean for a specified length of time, usually for one day (15:5-11, 19, 21-22, 27).

The rituals required for dealing with primary uncleanness varied according to whether the discharge was short-term or long-term. An emission of semen required washing and being subject to uncleanness for the rest of the day. Menstrual impurity remained in effect for seven days.

Long-term discharges were treated more seriously. When the discharge had ceased the one who was healed had to wait a week, wash, then the following day take two turtledoves or two pigeons to the priest, "to the entrance to the tent of meeting". The priest would offer one bird for a sin offering and the other for a burnt offering (15:13-15, 28-30).

After giving birth, the mother had to stay away from the Tabernacle and its holy things for thirty-three days if the child was a boy and for sixty-six days if the child was a girl. At the end of that time she had to bring a year-old lamb for a burnt offering and a turtle-dove or a pigeon for a sin offering. If she could not afford a lamb then she could bring two birds (12:6-8). The offerings required were the same whether the child was a son or a daughter (12:6,7).

The sin offering was not to gain forgiveness for any specific sins, but to acknowledge the uncleanness that the disease of sin brings, and to give assurance to the worshipper that, through the blood of the sacrifice, they were made clean. The burnt offering celebrated the fact that the period of uncleanness had come to an end. It re-established, through blood sacrifice, the worshipper's relationship with God which had been interrupted for the period of uncleanness.

Feminine Dignity

The period of uncleanness following an emission of semen was less than twenty-four hours but for menstruation it was seven days. This was in line with the times taken for the discharges to take place. Otherwise there was no difference in the procedures required for purification for men and for women. Women were treated equally with men.

It might seem unfair for a woman to be put out of circulation for one week in every four. But it could be looked upon as a loving way of relieving her of responsibilities while she would not be feeling at her best. It is also possible that the monthly period was not nearly so common in that culture as it is in the western world today. It was quite normal for a girl to be married at thirteen; large families were desirable so there might not be much time between pregnancies; it was usual to breastfeed until the child was three. All these factors could mean that a woman would menstruate relatively few times between getting married and the menopause.

The regulations made clear that sex was not a matter of demand and supply - for the man to demand and for the woman to supply. This was in direct contrast to the cultures of the surrounding nations. Before enjoying sexual intercourse, a God-fearing couple would consider carefully whether or not in the following twenty-four hours they were to be engaged in any service of God from which they would be barred. Being barred was not because sexual intercourse was considered sinful, but because it belonged to the realm of the "common" rather than to the "holy" (1 Samuel 21:4).

A God-fearing man would be aware of how close to menstruating his wife might be so as to avoid the possibility of being barred from God's service for seven days. In heathen nations a woman had to endure her husband's advances even during menstruation. In Israel such an action would result in the couple being "cut off from among their people" (20:18). So God's laws gave women dignity and protection.

The status of women in God's eyes is made clear in chapter 12. After giving birth and when the days of her purifying are completed, she must bring the sacrificial animals to the priest at the entrance to the tent of meeting (12:6 and 8). In the surrounding cultures only the men were involved in such sacred rituals. God not only allowed women to take part but commanded the mother to be directly involved in the sacrificial process.

Sons and Daughters

Why then is the mother unclean for twice as many days after the birth of a daughter as after the birth of a son? Why does it take twice as long for her to be purified?

If the reason was that daughters were of less value and so brought greater impurity than sons did, one would expect some mention to have been made of babies born deformed or seriously ill. Also, if the difference has to do with Eve's role in The Fall, one would expect to see a difference in the sacrifices required. But it is twice made clear that the sacrifices required are the same whether the child born is a son or a daughter (12:6 and 7).

70

As already noted, it is not the giving birth but her post-natal discharge that makes her ceremonially unclean. It may have been that the mother's vaginal discharge continued for longer after the birth of a daughter than after the birth of a son. There is no indication of that being the case in recent times.

On the eighth day, a son had to leave his mother's care, at least briefly, for circumcision (12:3). This was the first stage in the process of his being welcomed into the male community. By New Testament times sons were educated in matters of God's Law so that, at age thirteen, they could become full members of the synagogue. Meanwhile, daughters were taught by their mothers about house-keeping and raising a family. Proverbs 31:10-31 would seem to show that these were the priorities in Old Testament times. If such distinctions were already in place in the time of Moses, then the double times could have served to strengthen the bond between mother and daughter.

A daughter would eventually begin the menstrual cycle; she would in all probability one day herself give birth. So, in a sense, at the birth of a daughter two women were involved. It has been suggested that periods of uncleanness and purification of double the length of those for a son were an acknowledgement of that fact. They would, in fact, indicate how important daughters were for the continuing life of the nation and so how valuable they were.

A Special Occasion

Large families were the aim and the norm but each birth was treated as special. Giving birth and the days immediately following birth are physically dangerous for both mother and child and were especially so in those days. So it was important to be sure of God's care and protection by obeying God's laws. From a practical point of view, forty or eighty days out of circulation gave both of them time to recover, and gave the mother time to take particular care of her child.

Giving birth was also spiritually dangerous. A woman's son would one day, through His own suffering, inflict a fatal wound upon Satan (Genesis 3:15), who would try to prevent this and so make sure that his dominion over the world continued (Revelation 12:3-5). Every son born was the possible fulfilment of God's promise, so no time was to be lost in making him a member of the covenant community through circumcision (12:3). Every child born was potentially the ancestor of the one who would defeat Satan. So it was vital that

71

uncleanness was removed in order to re-establish and maintain that relationship with God and so ensure that that line was not "cut off"(22:3).

If uncleanness was not dealt with God's tabernacle would be defiled, and this would prove fatal for the people (15:31). And it was vital that the whole nation should be preserved. God's dealings with Israel in their history and through the prophets provided the backdrop which explained who Jesus was and made sense of what He said and did. It explained the victory of the Cross and the significance of the Resurrection. Without the Old Testament nobody would have known who Jesus was. So God provided the means of keeping the nation in fellowship with Himself, sometimes merely as a remnant (Isaiah 10:21), so that God's revelation of Himself and of His plan of salvation would be complete.

Reminders

Each one of the regulations about bodily purity was given by God and turned the Israelite's attention to God and His requirements. In that way each was a reminder of the One who is the ultimate source of life (Genesis 2:7) and who has ultimate control over both life and death (Genesis 2:16-17; Matthew 10:28). So the regulations implanted and perpetuated a conviction of the sanctity of human life. While they were a reminder of the seriousness of The Fall and its consequences (Genesis 3:16), the requirement of sacrifices would also give assurance that God would provide a way to deal with sin and death.

Jesus Our Healer

A woman who had had a discharge of blood for twelve years came to Jesus (Matthew 9:20-22; Mark 5:25-34; Luke 8:43-48). For twelve years she had been deprived of normal human society since everything and everybody she touched would have become unclean. For twelve years she had been barred from the synagogue, from the temple and from joining in any sacrificial feasts. In addition, the physicians she had consulted had taken all her money but their treatments had made her worse.

She had heard about the miracles Jesus had done for others and was convinced that even if she could only reach out to touch His clothes she would be healed. It must have taken some courage to push through the crowd. If there had been in the crowd those who knew she was unclean and was making them unclean by touching them the result could have been unpleasant. But she was right and the cure was instantaneous.

Jesus knew that power had gone out from Him but He told the woman that it was her faith that had made her well. Jesus has the power, she had the faith.

The law required that the woman would have to wait until she was healed before she could be restored to fellowship. Jesus did not abolish that law. He fulfilled it by providing the cure so that no-one need wait. This applies to the sin disease. Anyone who waits until they are good enough to come will never come. We come to Jesus for Him to make us good enough, to give us righteousness (right standing before God) as a gift (Romans 5:17) which He paid for by dying for us.

Most of the discharges of Leviticus 12 & 15 had to do with death or with the failure to produce life. This is a shadow of the reality that the disease called sin, with which we are all infected, is fatal (Romans 6:23). But those who believe in Jesus are so thoroughly healed that, though they die, they will live on forever (John 11:25-26). Even though the experience of Christians is like that of Paul, that the sin disease continues to show its symptoms when we do things that are displeasing to God (Romans 7:15), the law that sin will inevitably lead to death no longer applies; God has set us free from that (Romans 7:24-25). The law that now applies to believers is that the Spirit of God within those who are in Christ Jesus will inevitably lead to life (Romans 8:1-2).

Bodily Purity, Diseases and Moulds
Leviticus 13 and 14

What disease?

Most English versions of the Old Testament use words and phrases such as "leprosy", "plague of leprosy" or "leprous disease" to refer to the skin diseases (13:1-46; 14:1-32), the problems with fabrics and leather (13:47-59), and the growths on the walls of houses (14:33-53) with which the priest has to deal. This follows the Septuagint use of the Greek word *lepra* in these chapters.

But when the Greeks later came to refer specifically to what we know as leprosy, they used the word *elephantiasis*. They used *lepra* of any disease which produced flaky skin, so the word refers to a symptom rather than to a specific disease. The Hebrew it translates is a word which has to do with being struck and is at times explained by using the word for snow (Exodus 4:6; Numbers 12:10). This may be a reference to snow's whiteness, but it could also be a reference to snow being flaky, and this would account for the use of *lepra* by the Greek translators.

Some see possible references to specific skin complaints: psoriasis in 13:2-28, a fungal infection known as favus in 13:29-37, and vitiligo, also known as leucoderma (ESV 13:39), which is caused by skin pigment cells ceasing to function, in 13:38-39. Modern medical opinion is that, although several different complaints are included here, the defining symptoms of what we know as leprosy are not mentioned.

Another factor to consider is that the same Hebrew and Greek words are used of growths in fabrics and leather (13:47-59) and in the walls of houses (14:33-53). Leprosy is transmitted through mucus from the nose, not by infected fabric, leather or plaster. More modern English versions such as NIV and CEV use the word "mildew" in these passages.

The priest's task

It was not the task of the priest to diagnose and identify the particular disease. He was not like a modern GP having to make a specific diagnosis in order to prescribe the appropriate treatment. God gave these instructions to Moses and Aaron, not so that they could prescribe cures but so that they could separate the unclean from the clean and holy (10:10). The cure was in

74

God's hands. But if the people were not separated from their uncleanness, God's tabernacle would be defiled and that would be fatal (15:31).

Although the priest was responsible for deciding on matters of uncleanness, he was not to conduct a witch hunt. A diseased person was to be brought to the priest (13:2), or he might show himself to the priest (13:7). An article of fabric or leather was to be shown to the priest (13:49). The owner of a house with mildew was to go and tell the priest that there seemed to be a problem (14:35). So in the first instance, dealing with the problem was the responsibility of the individual Israelite.

Diagnosing Uncleanness

The first symptom the priest was to look for was discolouration either in hair and skin (13:3 et.al.), or in fabric and leather (13:49), or in the walls of houses (14:37). The next thing was to see whether or not the problem was superficial (13:3; 14:37).

In the case of a skin disease, if it was obviously more than skin deep, the priest was to pronounce the sufferer unclean without further tests (13:3). The other symptom which made the uncleanness of a person certain was the presence of raw flesh in the discoloured area (13:10, 14).

In most cases however, the decision to pronounce unclean was not made without making sure that the disease was actively spreading. To do so the person (13:4 et.al.), or the article (13:50), or the house (14:38) was put in quarantine for seven days.

If, after that time, examination by the priest showed that the skin disease had not spread, a further week of quarantine was imposed (13:5 and 33). If there was obvious improvement and the disease had not spread, the infected person was pronounced clean and simply had to wash their clothes (13:6). If, however, the disease had spread they were declared unclean (13:7-8).

In the case of an article of fabric or leather, if after one period of quarantine the mildew had spread, the article was burned (13:51-52). If the mildew had not spread (13:53), the article was to be washed and placed in quarantine for another seven days (13:54). If at the end of that time there was no improvement in the appearance of the mildew, the article was burned (13:55). If the mildew had faded, the infected part was torn out and burned (13:56), the article was washed again and considered clean (13:58). Any reappearance of the mildew would render the article unclean (13:57).

75

In the case of a house with mildew, if after seven days the disease had spread, the affected plaster and stones had to be removed and replaced (14:39-42). If the disease broke out again the whole house had to be destroyed (14:43-45).

So the main characteristics of uncleanness were discolouration, non-superficiality and persistent growth.

The Purpose

The modern attitude to disease tends to the assumption that the purpose was to preserve the physical health of the nation by preventing the spread of disease. But this cannot be the case with all the diseases referred to here. For example, if, as seems likely, the disease referred to in 13:2-28 is psoriasis, it is not contagious. And concern about the spread of disease from one person to another is not even hinted at in these chapters.

The reason for all the rules of chapters 12-15 is given in 15:31. That is, that unless the people of Israel and their uncleanness are separated, they will die. The purpose of these laws was to preserve the spiritual health of the nation rather than its physical health.

At creation God saw that the world he had made was very good (Genesis 1:31); it was perfect, complete and whole. These diseases and the mildew were abnormal and disfiguring. They destroyed the wholeness of God's creation; they were contrary to all that God had intended; they were incompatible with the presence of God in all his perfection. So, unless the uncleanness was removed, it would separate the people from God whose dwelling place was at the centre of the camp.

These are not medical regulations. They have to do with ceremonial uncleanness. They show what God says will separate his people from him, and what God says what must be done to preserve their fellowship with him.

Separation

Separating the people of Israel from uncleanness required drastic measures. If washing and tearing out the affected part in an article of fabric or leather failed to stem the spread of the mildew, then the whole article was burned (13:57). If removing and replacing infected stones and plaster failed to stem the spread of the mildew, then the whole house was demolished and the rubble was thrown outside the village or town (14:44-45).

Dealing with skin diseases was more painful. It was not merely the disease that was unclean; it was always the person with the disease who was to be pronounced unclean (13:3,8,11,15,20,22, 25,27,30,37,44). So the only means of separation was for the infected person to leave the community (13:45-46).

Tearing one's clothes was a sign of mourning (Genesis 37:34) or shame (Ezra 9:5-6). Leaving the hair unkempt and covering the lower part of the face were signs of mourning denied to Ezekiel at the death of his wife (Ezekiel 24:15-17). Crying, "Unclean!" was intended to warn others so that they did not become unclean by contact (7:21).

He or she had to live alone, that is, separated from family and friends and all the normal activities of life. It was a sort of living death. What did they do with themselves? Did they have to scavenge for food? Did family or friends leave food and water for them at a safe distance? The worst aspect for a God-fearing Israelite was that they were banished from God's presence - God dwelt at the centre, they were right outside.

Restoration

But there was hope of healing and restoration. Unlike the burning of a fabric or leather article and the demolition of a house, banishment was not necessarily permanent (13:46). The infected person was not sent right away but, "His dwelling shall be outside the camp." God in His grace might bring healing and provision was made for that (14:1-32).

Restoration to fellowship took place in three stages. The setting for the first stage was outside the camp (3-8a); for the second it was within the camp but outside the home tent (8b-9); for the third it was "at the entrance of the tent of meeting" (10-32). The banishment of an individual was a very serious matter and the rules had to be carefully observed. Equally, the reverse process of restoration was not to be undertaken lightly and the process God prescribed for it was slow and deliberate. In that respect it is worth noting that although the priest is to pronounce the individual clean towards the end of the first stage (7), he continues to be described as "the one to be cleansed" (8,11,14,17,18,25,28,29) until all the stages are complete. The reference in several instances to the number seven indicates that the cleansing was to be complete and perfect.

Stage one

The priest would be asked to examine the individual outside the camp (2-3). If healing was confirmed, the priest would arrange for the items required for the first cleansing ceremony to be brought out. These were two live clean birds, cedar wood, scarlet yarn, hyssop and an earthenware vessel containing fresh water (4-5). One of the birds was killed in such a way that its blood fell into the water (5). Then the priest took the remaining bird, together with all the other items, and dipped them into the blood and water (6). The priest sprinkled the blood and water seven times on the one to be cleansed, pronounced him clean then released the bird "into the open field" (7). The one being cleansed then had to wash his clothes, shave off all his hair and bathe himself before coming into the camp (8a).

The death of the one bird reminded the healed man of what his fate would have been if God had not intervened. The cedar wood and scarlet yarn, both red, would serve to emphasise the redness of the bird's blood. The roots of hyssop had a reputation for being able to penetrate rock and its use represented deep cleansing (Psalm 51:7). Fresh water was specified to ensure that no impurities were brought into the situation. The released bird symbolised the carrying far away of all the uncleanness that had resulted in the banishment (compare 16:20-22).

Stage two

For seven days the one to be cleansed had to live outside his tent (8b). On the seventh day he had to shave off all his hair, even his eyebrows, wash his clothes and bathe himself (9). In this way he would be on display to the community. Everyone would be able to see, especially as a result of the shaving, that he really was healed, and be assured that there was no cover-up.

Stage three

On the eighth day he had to go to the priest at the entrance of the tent of meeting taking with him the perfect animals required for sacrifice. For the one who could afford it these were one male lamb for a guilt offering, another male lamb for a sin offering and a year-old ewe lamb for a burnt offering (10). Those who were not so well off could bring a male lamb for a guilt offering and two turtledoves or two pigeons for the sin offering and burnt offering (21-22). Rich or poor, they had to bring about five pounds of fine flour mixed with oil for a grain offering, and half a pint of olive oil.

The one to be cleansed was "set before the LORD" together with the sacrifices he was about to offer (11). All the rituals were performed "before the LORD" (12,16,18,23,24,27,29,31). It was not the priest or the people who were being asked to accept the banished one back. He had been banished from God's presence, now it was for God to accept and restore.

That God required such offerings should not, in most cases, surprise us. The sin offering acknowledged that, ultimately if not directly, it was sin that had brought the disease. It also brought purification from that which had resulted in the banishment. The burnt offering re-established and re-affirmed the individual's relationship with God. The grain offering was a gift to God and a reminder of the covenant which God had made with His people, a covenant of privilege and of responsibility. These offerings combined to confirm the cleansing and restoration of the individual.

The unusual details of this series of offerings are those which involved the guilt offering. Unusually, it was to be offered first and so shown to be of special significance in those circumstances. And the same animal, a perfect male lamb, was required from both rich and poor.

The one to be cleansed may have wondered whether or not the disease had been due to his sin. The guilt offering would remove this sense of guilt (5:17-19).

During the period of banishment God had been deprived of the worship and service of that individual. That debt had to be paid by means of the guilt offering.

In addition the one being cleansed needed to be restored to the service of God from which he or she had been absent. The anointing with blood from the guilt offering (14,25) and with the oil (15-18,26-29) followed the same pattern as in Aaron's ordination. Some of the blood had been thrown against the altar (7:2), and the oil had been sprinkled seven times before the LORD (16,27). So the individual was closely linked to the altar and to the LORD Himself and, through these powerful symbols, was assured that he had been accepted back into God's service.

79

Skin diseases and sin

There is not always a direct connection between sin and sickness. Jesus made that clear when his disciples questioned him about the cause of a man's blindness (John 9:1-3). The uncleanness dealt with in Leviticus is not moral but ritual. The banishment was not by way of punishment but a means of separation. These laws are not about reality; they are not there to state that everyone with a skin disease is to be banished from God's presence, or that anything infected with mildew must be destroyed. They are "shadows of reality". They serve to illustrate that sin makes us unfit for God's presence and so separates us from Him.

When Adam and Eve disobeyed God they were driven out of Eden (Genesis 3:23-24) where they had until then enjoyed the presence of God. In Psalm 51, written after Nathan had confronted David about his adultery with Bathsheba, David shows that he was aware that he was in danger of being banished from God's presence (11). It is obvious that he had an overwhelming sense of the need to be made clean (2, 7), not just physically but in his heart (10).

Jesus Cleanses and Restores

When a leper came to Jesus for cleansing, He reached out and touched him (Matthew 8:2-4). The result was not that the contact made Jesus unclean but that the leper was made clean. Whenever Jesus' dealings with lepers is mentioned, the fact that He made them clean is emphasised (Matthew 11:4-5; Luke 17:14). These people, banished from society and from God's presence because of their ceremonially defiling skin diseases, were able to go and show themselves to the priest and be restored to fellowship with God and with family and friends.

Showing the priest that the disease had gone was not enough. Jesus told the leper to offer the sacrificial gift required by the Law. Restoration to fellowship with God requires sacrifice.

So it is with the defilement of sin. Jesus was able to tell the paralysed man that his sins were forgiven (Mark 2:5), but only because of the eternal value of the Cross. It is Jesus' blood, His death that cleanses (1 John 1:9). The multitude in heaven wear robes that are white because they have "washed their robes ... in the blood of the Lamb" (Revelation 7:9,14); they are clean because they are relying on Jesus' death for them.

80

Genesis 3 also demonstrates how sin separates people from each other. When confronted by God, Adam and Eve began to blame one another for what they had done. Jesus restores human relationships. "Simon the leper" (Matthew 26:6) had apparently suffered from a skin disease which had rendered him an outcast. Now he was at home and able to entertain guests so he must have been healed. Perhaps the fact that he had invited Jesus to a meal at his house indicates that it was Jesus who had healed him. Whatever the details, the story illustrates the truth that when Jesus deals with sin, when He forgives and cleanses, human relationships are restored.

There is a lesson here for Christian disciples. What John calls "walking in darkness", that is living a life that is characterised by wrong-doing, is incompatible with having fellowship with God (1 John 1:6). Conversely, "walking in the light", that is living a life that is characterised by doing what pleases God, results in us having "fellowship with one another" (1 John 1:7). At the same time the blood of Jesus God's Son cleanses us from the sin that is an inherent part of our nature, and, being cleansed, we will have fellowship with God, Father and Son. So fellowship with God and fellowship with one another are both parts of the one thing and dependent both on the blood of Jesus and the lives we live.

Caring for the environment

The laws about mildew in articles of fabric or leather, and in houses illustrate the fact that human sin affects our environment. The cleansing ceremony for a house (14:49-53) was the same as the initial cleansing ceremony for a banished individual (14:4-7). This indicates that the ceremonial uncleanness was of the same kind in each case. Human sin affects our environment.

That our misuse of the natural world and its resources has done great and sometimes irreparable damage is beyond dispute. Not everyone would accept that if we had treated the world according to God's laws the damage would not have been done.

Our environment is more than what we might call the world of nature. It includes our society, our culture. Ungodliness pervades our society. The way bankers operate, the way corners are cut in manufacture, the attitude that making a profit is the most important thing, all show that our environment has been and is being ruined by sin. Christians have a responsibility to exert an

81

influence in the opposite direction. Paul told the Christians at Philippi that they were living in a "crooked and twisted generation", and called on them to "shine as lights in the world" (Philippians 2:15).

The Day of Atonement
Leviticus 16

Purpose

It was inconceivable that the whole nation could continue for long without some of them unwittingly offending against the purity laws of chapters 11-15. Those who did so were rendered ritually unclean. Equally, it was inconceivable that the whole nation could continue for long without some of them unintentionally offending against the moral laws. This is particularly so if we bear in mind what Jesus revealed about the impossibly high standard of morality that God really required (Matthew 5:21-22, 27-28). So the purpose of the Day of Atonement was not only to deal with ritual uncleanness, but also to deal with "iniquities", "transgressions" and "sins" (16, 21). It was to take place once a year on the tenth day of the seventh month (29) like an annual spring clean.

Style

This chapter has been written in such a way that the exact order of events is not immediately obvious. For example, the instruction is given in verse 6 that Aaron is to offer a bull as a sin offering for himself and his family. Then that is repeated, after instructions about two goats, in verse 11. Using one of the goats as a sin offering is mentioned in verse 9, then the instruction to kill it is given in verse 15.

It may help to understand the chapter if verses 6 to 10 are taken as an outline of the events which are then described in detail in verses 11 to 28.

Precautions

If anyone approached the tent of meeting while unclean they would be cut off from God's presence (22:3). So the rituals of this special day were to be carried out by Aaron as high priest on his own (17), and even he had to take great care. There was only one way he could approach God (3) and that was to follow these instructions which God gave to Moses. Nadab and Abihu had evidently entered God's presence carelessly and arrogantly and, as a result, had died (10:1-2). So Aaron had to prepare carefully and take certain precautions to ensure that he did not suffer the same fate.

Preparation

Aaron had to remove his splendid high-priestly robes, bathe himself and put on simple garments of linen, a coat secured with a sash, an undergarment and a turban. In his high-priestly robes he would have appeared to the people to be like a king, but he was to enter God's presence dressed as a humble servant. Bathing would have symbolised the genuine, inner purity which God required.

He had to assemble the animals that were required for sacrifice. These were a bull and a ram for himself and his family (3, 6), and two goats and a ram for the people (5).

The two goats were "set before the LORD" and God decided, through the casting of lots, which of them would be "for the LORD" and which would be "for Azazel" (7-8).

The goat that was "for the LORD" was sacrificed by Aaron as a sin offering for the people (9, 15). He was also to sacrifice the bull as a sin offering for himself and his family (6, 11).

Aaron had to put live coals from the altar in a censer, and have ready two handfuls of incense.

Applying the Blood

Aaron was to take the censer and the incense, some of the blood from the sacrificed bull and the sacrificed goat, across the courtyard, through the Holy Place, then on through the veil into the Most Holy Place. There he was to put the incense on the fire in the censer so that the smoke from it would cover the mercy seat, the lid of the Ark. It was from above the mercy seat that God said he would meet with Moses and speak with him (Exodus 25:22). But God also told Moses that no-one could see him and live (Exodus 33:20). By covering the mercy seat with smoke from the incense God's presence would be hidden from Aaron and he would not die (12-13).

He was to dip his finger in the blood of the bull, sprinkle it on the mercy seat, then sprinkle it seven times in front of the mercy seat. He was to repeat this with the blood of the goat (15). Leaving the Most Holy Place, Aaron had to sprinkle blood from the two animals in the Holy Place (16). He then went across the courtyard to the altar where he applied blood from both animals to its horns (18). In this way he would be making atonement for the Holy Place (16), for the tent of meeting (16) and for the altar (18). The application of the blood would remove the nation's uncleannesses, transgressions, iniquities and sins from God's holy things. This would maintain the Tent of Meeting in a fit state for God to dwell in.

The Scapegoat

Aaron had then to go to the entrance to the tent of meeting where the live goat was waiting. He would "present" the live goat (20), that is, all that he did with the live goat was done at God's command, in God's sight and for God to approve and accept. He had to lay both his hands on the head of the goat and confess over it "all the iniquities of the people of Israel, and all their transgressions, all their sins" (21). A man was to be waiting ready to lead the goat away from all habitation and to release it into the wilderness (22).

The two goats together made up one sin offering (5); together they achieved one result, the removal of the defilement from all Israel's uncleannesses and sins. The blood of the first goat was used, along with the blood of the bull, to cleanse all God's holy things (33) from defilement. Aaron had been appointed to bear any guilt incurred by the people of Israel (Exodus 28:38). The picture on the Day of Atonement seems to be that Aaron cleansed all defilement from God's holy things, then bore all that defilement out to the entrance and put it all on the head of the goat (21). He was to use both hands (21), perhaps to make it clear that every particle of all the defilement he was carrying was transferred to the goat.

God had chosen this goat "for Azazel". The meaning of "Azazel" is uncertain. It could be the name of a demon thought to occupy desert places and the significance might be that all sins were sent back to their author where they belonged. But the scapegoat was certainly not to be regarded as a sacrifice to a demon (17:7). The word may mean "a rocky precipice" down which the goat fell or was pushed to its death.

Whatever the people understood by the word, the outcome was the important thing. The goat, along with its burden of uncleannesses and sins, left the camp never to return. God was removing their sins "as far as the east is from the west" (Psalm 103:12). It would have the same effect as if he had thrown all their sins into the deepest part of the sea (Micah 7:19).

Returning to Normal

After laying his hands on the live goat, Aaron had to re-enter the tent of meeting. He had to remove the plain linen garments (23), bathe himself and put on his high priestly robes (24) in order to resume his normal duties as high priest. On this day these duties were to offer the burnt offerings for priests and people (24) and to burn the fat of the sin offerings (25). The remains of the bull and the goat were disposed of in the normal way (27; see 4:11-12).

The return to normal required washing. In Aaron's case this may have been in order to make a clean break from the activities of this exceptional day. There was to be no question of him thinking that by having entered God's presence he was in any way special because of that, or that he could enter God's presence whenever he wished. This is emphasised by the command to leave the linen clothes in the tent of meeting (23). A year would pass before God allowed the high priest to pass beyond the veil again, and he would then have to make the same careful preparations and take the same precautions.

The one who had led away the goat had to wash his clothes and bathe (26) before re-entering the camp. The same rules applied to the one who dealt with the remains of the sin offerings (28). There was to be no hint of the possibility of defilement being brought back into the camp.

True Repentance

The rituals of that day were to involve, not just the high priest and the one who led away the scapegoat and the one who dealt with the remains of the sin offerings. The whole nation was to be involved. This was the one day in the year when they would be clean in God's sight (30). Every individual had to demonstrate that, although they were not directly involved in the sacrifices, they were taking it seriously, they were admitting their need for cleansing and wanting to be right with God, and they were honouring what was being done on their behalf. They were to do so by making the day special by not working. They were not allowed to get foreigners living among them to do their work for them. The Day was more important than anything else. It was even more important than their own needs. So they were to "afflict" themselves (29-31), that is, they were to deny themselves.

Denying themselves would have involved fasting at least. On one occasion David's self-affliction included wearing sackcloth, fasting and praying (Psalm 35:13). He did this because he was grieving over the suffering of others, and he was denying himself in order to pray for them. God demands that displays of self-denial are accompanied by treating others well, otherwise it is sheer hypocrisy (Isaiah 58:3-7). By such behaviour the Israelites were to show true repentance and so benefit from the cleansing that was being worked out for them on that day.

True repentance is not only an attitude to the past. It is also a returning to God and His ways. The burnt offerings which Aaron offered towards the end of the day made atonement (24). They re-established the fellowship between God and His people and symbolised a rededication of the lives of priests and people to God.

A Permanent Requirement

The phrase "a statute forever" is applied in the Pentateuch to fifteen different aspects of the ritual law. It is used three times (29, 31, 34) of the Day of Atonement. And yet, as already noted, these rituals are no more than shadows of reality (Colossians 2:17). In what sense then were these rituals to be permanent?

The writer of Hebrews says, "It is impossible for the blood of bulls and goats to take away sins" (Hebrews 10:4). Yet the rituals and sacrifices of the Day of Atonement were evidently effective, since God's presence continued with His people as long as the regulations were observed with true repentance. They were effective because of the obedient faith of the people and because of the reality to which they pointed forward. They pointed forward to the time when the Day of Atonement would be fulfilled at the Cross. The Cross was erected and endured in Time, but it stands in eternity and its effects remain in Eternity forever. God's command that the shadow which is the Day of Atonement should be permanent is fulfilled in the reality of the Cross of Christ.

The Perfect Fulfilment

Christ fulfilled Aaron's role of high priest. He did so, not by being merely another of Aaron's descendants who took over the work when their fathers passed away (Leviticus 16:32). He is High Priest by virtue of his "indestructible life" (Hebrews 7:16), that is His resurrection life. So he is High Priest forever (Hebrews 7:21, 24). Aaron and his descendants entered a man-made replica of God's dwelling place. Christ has entered into heaven itself. There, without any need for smoke from incense to protect Him, He remains in the presence of God continuing His work on our behalf (Hebrews 9:24).

He fulfilled the sacrifices of the Day of Atonement even to the disposing of the remains of the sin offerings by suffering outside the city (Hebrews 13:11-12). But, unlike Aaron, He did not have to offer sacrifices for Himself (Hebrews 7:26-28). The sacrifice He offered was the sacrifice of Himself (Hebrews 9:12).

This sacrifice is effective not only for outward, ritual cleansing but to cleanse the conscience, that is, to provide inward cleansing so that the believer is brought into fellowship with God (Hebrews 9:14).

He fulfilled the part of the scapegoat. There are no explicit statements in the New Testament linking the work of Christ to the scapegoat. There are, however, several passages where the writers use the idea of Jesus carrying away our sins. He was made sin for our sake (2 Corinthians 5:21); He "bore our sins in His body on the cross" (1 Peter 2:24); the purpose of His sacrifice was to take away the sins of many (Hebrews 9:28). This may also be part of what John the Baptist had in mind when he referred to Jesus as "the lamb of God who takes away the sin of the world" (John 1:29)

Christ fulfilled every aspect of the Day of Atonement in such a way that the work need never be repeated. Aaron and his descendants had to repeat the same ceremonies year after year. But by offering Himself as a perfect sinless sacrifice, Jesus entered into God's presence once for all time and for all who will believe; the redemption He secured is eternal (Hebrews 9:12).

The effect of Christ's work goes far beyond anything achieved by the Old Testament high priests or hoped for by the people. Not only has Jesus entered into God's presence Himself, He has also made a way in for us. This is hinted at in the gospels where they tell of how, at the moment when Jesus died, the curtain, beyond which only the high priest was allowed to pass once a year, was torn in two from top to bottom (Mark 15:38). Now "we have confidence to enter the holy places by the blood of Jesus" (Hebrews 10:19) and we are encouraged to "draw near" (Hebrews 9:22). Because of Jesus' death we can enter God's presence at any time and there find the help we need (Hebrews 4:16).

The Appropriate Response

The way into God's presence has been opened for us at great cost (Hebrews 10:19-21), so we are called to take advantage of that great privilege (Hebrews 10:22). We may draw near to God by prayer, by responding to his Word with obedient faith and by the way we live. We must do so with confidence knowing that by the blood of Christ our hearts have been made clean. As was the case with the washing carried out on the Day of Atonement, the washing of our bodies in baptism is an outward symbol of inner cleansing,

88

and the remembrance of that event can give us confidence that the inner cleansing has taken place (Hebrews 10:22).

We are assured that when we draw near to God, He will draw near to us (James 4:8). We must draw near with our faith focused on Jesus alone, completely confident that He will keep His promises (Hebrews 10:23).

We must draw near "with a true heart", that is, in perfect sincerity (Hebrews 10:22). In Isaiah's time the people of Judah were appearing before God in so far as they were coming to the temple with their sacrifices. But God asked, "Who has required of you this trampling of my courts?" (Isaiah 1:12). It was "trampling" because they were performing religious rituals without abandoning their evil ways (Isaiah 1:13). We cannot enter God's presence while clinging on to favourite sins.

The Israelites were called to self-denial especially on the Day of Atonement. The Lord Jesus said that those who wished to be His disciples must deny themselves (Mark 8:34). Christians are called to self-denial in order to serve others. We must do all we can to avoid causing others to stumble (Romans 14:21). Instead we must encourage them to live lives characterised by love and good works (Hebrews 10:24). To do this we need to keep on meeting together (Hebrews 10:25) in order to help one another to steer clear of living lives characterised by deliberate sinning (Hebrews 10:26).

Those to whom the Letter to the Hebrews was addressed had found that being Christians was most unpopular (Hebrews 10:32-34). The writer reminds them that, just as the remains of the sin offerings were burned outside the camp, so Jesus suffered outside the city. We are called to leave the camp of popularity and "bear the reproach he endured" (Hebrews 13:11-13), to follow Him whatever others think of us or do to us.

Blood and Life
Leviticus 17

A Connecting Link

Holiness in chapters 1-16 is to do with the rituals that take place in the tabernacle. Holiness in the following chapters is mainly to do with ethical matters in everyday life. Whereas the first part of Leviticus deals with the work and responsibilities of priests, the second part deals mainly with the responsibilities of the laity. Chapters 18 to 20 and 23 to 27 begin with a command to Moses to speak to the people of Israel. Chapters 21 & 22 are addressed to the priests but are a call to them to be holy in their personal lives, and the chapters show how personal holiness affects the practice of their profession. So chapters 18-27 have to do with personal holiness whether a person is of the laity or of the priesthood.

Chapters 18-26 are sometimes referred to as the Holiness Code because of the frequent use of the word holy, especially in the repeated call to the Israelites to be holy because the LORD their God is holy. Chapter 17 does not contain the word holy, but it does form a connecting link between chapters 1-16 and chapters 18-27. "Aaron and his sons" are included along with "all the people of Israel" in the address. And it links what is done at home (3), outside the camp (3) and when hunting (13) with the rituals of the tent of meeting (4-6, 9).

Terminating Idolatry

At Sinai, God had commanded that, if the Israelites were to be His people, they should have and serve only the one God, the LORD (Exodus 19:5; 20:3). But it seems that the Israelites had been conducting their own sacrifices "in the open field" (5), and that in doing so they were sacrificing "to goat demons" (7). It was commonly believed, especially among nomadic people, that goat demons lived in the wilderness and must be placated to ensure that travelling through their domain could be done in safety.

For God's people, to sacrifice to demons was worse than a wife being unfaithful to her husband; it was as if the Israelites were prostituting themselves (7). God's way of correcting the error and terminating the idolatry was to make it clear that all sacrifices were to be made only at the entrance to the tent of meeting (4). They were to be gifts "to the LORD", at the tabernacle "of the LORD", brought "to the LORD", as peace offerings "to the LORD", the

90

blood to be thrown on the altar "of the LORD", the burning of the fat to provide a pleasing aroma "to the LORD". So six times in verses 4-6 it is emphasised that sacrifices were to be made to the God to whom they belonged and only to Him.

Domestic Butchering

What was permitted in the way of slaughtering for domestic consumption? What were the rules that applied to animals unfit for sacrificing to the LORD? In Deuteronomy 12:20-25 the Israelites are clearly told that, when they settle in Canaan, they may eat meat whenever they wish provided they drain off the blood. Since the prohibitions of Leviticus 17 relate specifically to ritual killing for sacrifice, there is no reason to suppose that the rules of Deuteronomy concerning butchering for domestic use did not apply in the wilderness.

The Seriousness of Shedding Blood

The one who persists in offering sacrifices other than at the tabernacle will be "cut off from among his people" (4). This punishment is linked, not directly to the idolatry, but to the fact that the offender has "shed blood" (4).

After the Flood, just as God had previously given plants to mankind for food (Genesis 2:9, 16), so he then gave animals (Genesis 9:3-6). But this permission came with the restriction that the blood must first be drained from the flesh. The reason given is that the blood is the life. God immediately went on to speak, as it were "in the same breath", of the killing of humans. This is especially serious because man is made in God's image. But, for both man and animals, the blood is the life and life belongs to God.

It is against this historical background that the commands of Leviticus 17 are given. Anyone who killed an animal without acknowledging that its life belonged to God, especially in idol worship, was guilty of bloodshed (4). This was as serious as murder and they would be "cut off". Ensuring that sacrifices were made at the tent of meeting so that the blood was thrown on the altar of the LORD (6) was an acknowledgement that life belongs to God.

Consuming Blood Forbidden

The same punishment of being "cut off" was to be suffered by anyone who ate blood (10). As already noted, this restriction dates back to the time immediately after the Flood. When any animal was killed its blood was to be drained off before the meat was eaten. This applied to any animal killed when hunting (13). It also meant that eating the flesh of any animal that had died of natural causes or been killed by a predator should be avoided (15-16) since its corpse might still contain blood.

The reason given for not consuming blood was in two parts. The first was to reiterate the statement of Genesis 9:4 that the blood of an animal is its life (11). This statement would seem logical since loss of blood would result in loss of life. The second part of the reason was that God had given it to his people to make atonement, and that atonement was to be made on God's altar (11).

When going through survival training in Mexico a bullock was slaughtered for us to butcher. The animal was stunned, then an artery was cut and the blood drained off. This was given to the local Indians who prized it as being highly nourishing. But the blood was not given to the Israelites for their physical nourishment; it was given for their spiritual well-being. It was given so that a life might be given in a sinner's place, to restore relationships between God and his people, and to cleanse and purify from the defilement of sin.

Being Cut Off

No explanation is given of what it means to be cut off. In some modern versions of the Old Testament it is presented as meaning that the offender would or should no longer be considered as one of God's people. That would certainly have been serious enough because it would have meant being separated from all God's blessings and protection.

But the Hebrew word belongs in the realm of agriculture in which a plant would be said to have been "cut off" when it had been cut down. So it would seem to indicate a direct and final punishment rather than simply being deprived of blessing. Furthermore, in 17:10 and 20:3-6 it is clear that cutting off is something that God himself does. In view of this, sudden death, childlessness, or being denied a place in the after-life are some of the suggestions that have been made as to what being cut off might involve. If this is what the Israelites understood by the saying, the warning would serve as a strong deterrent. Although one's fellow Israelites might be totally unaware of one's offence, nothing is hidden from God (Psalm 139:1-4; Hebrews 4:13) and it is impossible to escape from him (Psalm 139:7-12).

So it was made clear that offending against life blood was very serious. This was reinforced by the fact that foreigners were included in the prohibitions of this chapter. Foreigners were permitted to live among the

Israelites and, it would seem, were to some extent allowed to follow their own customs and culture. For instance, they did not have to be circumcised but, if uncircumcised, they were not allowed to eat the Passover (Exodus 12:48). However, sacrificing to idols (8) and eating blood (10) were forbidden to them on pain of being cut off. This is not surprising since the vital importance of blood was originally made clear, not just to the Israelite nation, but at the re-start of the whole human race after the Flood.

The Exclusiveness of God

That there is only one God is clearly seen in the account of creation, which means that fact applies to all mankind. That God alone should be worshipped was confirmed by Jesus in his answer to Satan (Matthew 4:10), and when he said that the first and great commandment was to love God with all one's heart, soul and mind (Matthew 22:37-38). Although Paul agreed with the Christians in Corinth that "an idol has no real existence" (1 Corinthians 8:4), he went on to say that sacrifices made in idol worship were in fact being offered to demons (1 Corinthians 10:20). He warns them that they cannot have fellowship with the Lord while at the same time having fellowship with demons (1Corinthians 10:21).

Modern idolatry is more subtle. Paul said that the love of money is the root of all kinds of evil (1 Timothy 6:10) and that craving for wealth had led some to wander from the faith and to be pierced with pangs of disillusionment. He urges Timothy instead to pursue righteousness, godliness, faith, love, steadfastness and gentleness and to "fight the good fight of the faith". Things such as a career and the longing to be rich, or anything that takes God's place, are idols. It has been the aim of the evil one from the time in Eden (Genesis 3:6) to use such idols to draw people away from God. Jesus said, "You cannot serve God and money" (Matthew 6:24). Christ the Lord demands nothing less than total commitment from those who would follow him (Matthew 10:37).

In his first letter, John's final appeal to his readers is that they keep themselves from idols (1 John 5:21). Paul expressed the same concern (1 Corinthians 10:14).

The Sanctity of Life

The sanctity of life is also universally applicable. It is made very plain at creation that life belongs to God. He "breathed into man's nostrils the breath of

93

life" (Genesis 2:7). The psalmist addresses God as the source of all life (Psalm 36:9).

What is more, every person is made in the image of God (Genesis 1:26-27). This is what makes human life so precious (Genesis 9:6). Since a human being bears the image of God, their person, as well as their life, demands respect. As Jesus explained, to be angry with someone, to insult them or to call them a fool is to be liable to the same judgement as a murderer (Matthew 5:22).

The sanctity of human life is particularly pertinent when abortion, euthanasia or embryo research is being considered. If the facts that life is God's gift and that humans are made in His image are rejected, then it all comes down to human opinions and anything goes.

The Abortion Act of 1967 was passed to avoid a few hundred back-street abortions performed each year. Since then the annual rate of abortion has risen to more than 200,000 in the UK, many of them being repeat abortions, some women having as many as seven. Every abortion is a life destroyed.

The pressure to legalise euthanasia is relentless. As an eminent lawyer has said, the generation that killed their children will be killed by their children.

No-one knows what the outcome of embryo research will be.

The Consumption of Blood

At the conclusion of the Council of Jerusalem a letter was sent to the Gentile churches requiring them to abstain from what had been sacrificed to idols and from blood (Acts 15:28-29). This was a compromise intended to satisfy the Jewish Christians who wanted Gentile Christians to observe the whole Mosaic Law (Acts 15:5). In towns throughout the Roman Empire animals were slaughtered in sacrifices to idols and the meat was either eaten in the idol temple or it was sold. No great care was taken to ensure that the blood was drained from the carcasses. So the only way Gentile Christians could be sure to abide by the requirements of that letter would be to do their own slaughtering.

The Christians in Corinth asked Paul about eating meat offered to idols. His answer covers three chapters (1 Corinthians 8-10). His main concern was that they should not give offence to their fellow-believers (8:9). He tells them to avoid being associated with idol worship by eating in an idol's temple (8:10; 10:14). But he tells them they may buy whatever is on sale without asking questions about its history (10:25), and they may accept invitations to eat with unbelievers (10:27) without quizzing their hosts about the food they were being offered. However, although they had the right to do these things (8:9), they must always be ready to avoid giving offence (10:28-32).

The same principles apply in other matters where there are differences of opinion among Christians about what is permissible.

Christ's Blood and Life

Evidently Paul, although brought up as a strict Jew (Philippians 3:5), had come to see that there is nothing intrinsically wrong in consuming blood. When Paul met Jesus on the road to Damascus he began to see everything from a different point of view, that is, from Christ's point of view. See for example 2 Corinthians 5:16 where Paul is saying that, among other distinctions he used to make, he no longer distinguishes between Jews and Gentiles, between those who observe the Mosaic Law and those who do not.

The awesome respect for blood that God demanded of His people in the Law was pointing towards the Cross when the Son of God would pour out His lifeblood. With that Old Testament background in view, the enormous value of the blood of Christ may be appreciated. Jesus reaffirmed the equation between blood and life but, instead of reiterating the ban on consuming blood, He gave an invitation to drink His blood. He explained that those who do not drink His blood have no life in them (John 6:53-55).

Of course, this is symbolic. We need to accept Christ into our hearts, into our innermost beings, if we are to be alive to God. Communion is a regular reminder of this. At the Last Supper, as Jesus passed the cup round He said, "This is my blood of the covenant, which is poured out for many for the forgiveness of sins" and He asked all His disciples to drink of it (Matthew 26:27-28).

God gave the blood of animals to His people so that they could use it to make atonement for themselves (Leviticus 17:11) by offering it upon God's altar. God loved the world like this: He gave His only Son so that those who believe in Him may have eternal life (John 3:16). The Son of God loved me and gave Himself for me (Galatians 2:20). "God presented Christ as a sacrifice of atonement, through the shedding of His blood--to be received by faith" (Romans 3:25 NIV). God gave the blood of animals to His people; they had to use it. God has given the blood of His Son; each individual has to accept it for themselves.

Family Life
Leviticus 18

God's Best

In a society that regards personal choice and human rights as of first importance, this chapter is probably the least popular of the whole Bible. It is particularly detested by the homosexual community. Why should one's enjoyment of life be spoiled by the dictates of a God whose very existence is doubted or totally rejected?

The God of the Bible is not a spoilsport but one who wants the very best for His people. Of all the trees in the Garden of Eden, only one was forbidden. In creation God has provided all mankind's needs.

Sometimes rebellion against God's commands is due to a lack of understanding. The psalmist said that the more he understood of God's commandments the more eager he became to obey them (Psalm 119:32). In the same Psalm the writer says that he found great freedom in obeying God's laws (Psalm 119:45). James refers to God's law as "the law of liberty" (James 2:12).

The aim of the rules in Leviticus 18 was to produce strong families, because the family is the foundation stone of a stable society. The problems existing in the UK which are caused by the break-up of families are obvious. According to a report issued in 2009 by the Institute of Education at London University, family breakdown has a damaging effect on a child's educational achievement, their behaviour, their mental health, the way they view themselves, their ability to react acceptably with others and their long-term health. Add to this the increased risk of physical and sexual abuse in broken families, and the cost to society in dealing with all these problems, and it may be imagined what a society would be like if the actions condemned in this chapter were the norm.

The Way of Life

On the other hand, obedience to God's laws leads to fullness of life (5). Because of their disobedience, Adam and Eve were driven from Eden with its plentiful supply of all they needed. They were separated from God, the very source of life. To Israel God promised (26:3-9) that, if they would observe his commandments, he would ensure that the rains would come in season so that the land would be fertile and trees would bear fruit. He would protect them

97

from enemies and wild animals and they themselves would multiply. The prophets proclaimed the same message in one form or another (Ezekiel 20:11, 21).

God's Reason

To make happiness, satisfaction and fulfilment one's aims can be fatal, as Eve found (Genesis 3:6). God doesn't say, as some parents do to their children, "I just want you to be happy and fulfilled." God's reason for giving these commands is expressed in the words, "I am the Lord your God", spoken in verse 2 and repeated five times (4, 5, 6, 21, 30). This is God's world and we are His creatures. He knows what is best and has every right to demand the obedience of His people. He is God.

For Israel there was much more to that statement than simply to say that God must be obeyed because He is God. The most significant time when God gave His name, "I am the LORD", was to Moses at the Burning Bush. God went on to promise that He would rescue the Hebrews from slavery (Exodus 3:14-17), which promise He kept. The giving of the Ten Commandments begins with the statement, "I am the LORD your God, who brought you out of the land of Egypt, out of the house of slavery" (Exodus 20:2). The reason God expected His people to obey His laws was because of what He had done for them. He rescued them from slavery. They did not deserve it; He did what He did because He loved them (Deuteronomy 7:7-8). He is not only God, but He says, "I am ... your God."

This was not a democracy. There was no discussion leading to a majority vote. The Hebrew words for "rules" and "statutes" emphasise the fact that they were given. Israel was expected to keep them, not because they agreed with them, but because they had been given by their God who had done so much for them.

The Alternative

The Hebrews had lived in Egypt for about 400 years, so succeeding generations had grown up knowing what the Egyptians believed about sex. It would not be surprising if they had come to think of Egyptian behaviour as the norm.

Some of the eighty gods of Egypt were simply gods of lust. In the royal family brothers married their sisters. Bestiality was approved and practised. At one time there was an area of the country in which women cohabited with

98

goats, and Ramses II claimed to be a son of Ptah, a god thought to take the form of a goat. So Israel needed to be told from the outset (3) that they were not to follow the Egyptians' example.

This command is immediately followed by the warning that when they entered Canaan they were not to behave as its inhabitants did. The Canaanites deified sex. Homosexuality, bestiality and the use of cult prostitutes, both male and female, were all encouraged in the belief that by doing so the gods would be persuaded to grant fertility in crops, flocks, herds and human offspring.

The behaviour of Egyptians and Canaanites was directed by what heathen gods supposedly demanded of their worshippers. By following the example of heathen nations the Israelites would be worshipping and obeying heathen gods. Not only must they reject their behaviour but, God says, "You shall follow my rules and keep my statutes and walk in them. I am the Lord your God" (4).

Forbidden Sexual Relationships

Sexual relationships with close relatives is forbidden (6). The words translated "close relatives" mean literally "flesh of his flesh". It includes those often referred to in western cultures as one's own flesh and blood: mother (7), sister (9), half-sister (9), granddaughter (10) and aunt (12, 13).

It is curious that daughters are not mentioned here. The reason may be that the result of Lot having sex with his daughters (Genesis 19:30-38) was that they gave birth to what became two of Israel's greatest enemies, Moab and Ammon. Moab tried to prevent Israel from approaching the Promised Land (Numbers 22-24). The Ammonites were persistently hostile from the time of the Judges (Judges 3:13) and on into the time of the Exile (Ezekiel 25:3). Perhaps with these constant reminders, Israel did not need to be told that having sex with one's daughter would lead to trouble.

Other relations listed here are not so obviously one's own flesh and blood: step-mother (8), step-sister (11), wife of an uncle (14), daughter-in-law (15), brother's wife (16), a step-brother's daughter (17), and a step-sister's daughter (17). They are included because, in the culture of the day, those brought into a family by marriage were considered to have entered into relationships with the members of that family as close as those actually born into that family. This is affirmed by the statement that when a man and a woman marry they "become

99

one flesh" (Genesis 2:23-24). A woman, when she married into a family became a daughter of that family (Ruth 3:1), and, for example, she also became a sister to her husband's brother. So having sex with these relations was also forbidden.

The rule of verse 16 assumes that the brother is still alive. If a man died leaving his widow childless, the brother was commanded to assume the duties of a husband to the widow in order to produce offspring, so that the name and line of the deceased would not die out (Deuteronomy 25:5-10).

Special Cases

The problems arising from having more than one wife are illustrated by the story of Hannah (1 Samuel 1). The problems would be magnified if the two women were sisters, as was the case with Leah and Rachel (Genesis 30). So the practice is prohibited here (18) because of the rivalry that would result.

The warning that having sex with a woman who is menstruating results in uncleanness (15:24) is here repeated as a prohibition (19). The commandment not to commit adultery (Exodus 20:14) is also repeated here (20).

The worship of Molech (21) was conducted in the Valley of Hinnom at the foot of the mount on which Jerusalem stands. It is thought that an idol of Molech would have been in the form of a giant with a bull's head. Each image had a hole in the abdomen and possibly outstretched arms making a ramp to the hole. Some illustrations show the image as hollow with a fire burning inside. Babies were placed in the statue's arms, or in the hole, and burnt. It is not certain whether they were killed first or burnt alive.

The worship of Molech had sexual connotations in two ways. The first is related to the fact that the prime purpose of sexual intercourse is procreation. In worshipping Molech, the couple would sacrifice their firstborn, the result of their intercourse, in the belief that Molech would ensure that more children would be given to them. The other factor was that the consort of Molech was Ashtoreth, the main fertility goddess of Canaan, the worship of whom involved cult prostitution. The worship of these two gods went hand in hand.

To worship Molech in this way would profane God's name (21), that is, God's reputation would be destroyed because Israel would have made Him seem to the world to be no different to heathen gods. But Israel had no need to resort in desperation to those fertility rites. They could and should simply trust their loving God to provide.

The practice of homosexuality is forbidden (22). From the beginning (Genesis 1:27-28; 2:24-25) the Scriptures present heterosexual marriage as the norm. One of the signs of the depraved state of Sodom was the desire of the men to have sex with Lot's male visitors (Genesis 19:1-29).

The ban on homosexual practice is not linked especially to idolatry any more than are the other prohibitions. The reason given is that it is "an abomination", that is, something that is totally disgusting to God. The aim of Leviticus 18 is to ensure healthy families, and homosexual practice would not help achieve that.

Bestiality is forbidden (23). Of all the ways in which the sex drive is misused, this one, more than any other, reduces humans to mere animals.

Accountability

The laws of Leviticus, including chapter 18, were given to those who were already God's people. They were to obey them because they were his people and as an expression of gratitude for all that he had done for them. But the rules of this chapter did not apply to Israel alone. The right purpose and practice of sex was established at Creation when God created mankind "male and female" and told them, "Be fruitful and multiply." The moral laws of God apply to the whole human race and offenders of whatever nationality are subject to his judgement. The prophets continued to proclaim this (Isaiah 13:11; Amos 1:3, 6, 9, et.al.).

Abuses of sex counted as "abominations" when practised by foreigners living within the community of Israel (26) and by foreign nations in their own lands. The people of Canaan were being judged by God in that He was driving them out of the land (24). God would use His people to drive them out (Numbers 33:50-52). But the picture here (25) is of the land itself, finding the behaviour of the inhabitants so disgusting, already beginning to retch and vomit in order to rid itself of the offence. Israel is warned that, if they adopt Canaanite behaviour, they too will be vomited out (26-28).

God's laws are so built in to creation that nature itself revolts at sin. We see this today, for example, in the spread of HIV/AIDS and other sexually transmitted diseases.

Leviticus 18 and the New Testament

The first Christians were Jews and thought that they must continue to observe the Law of Moses in every detail. They wanted to impose that on Gentile Christians. That issue was debated at the Council of Jerusalem (Acts 15) and a compromise was reached which served to avoid a split in the Church. But, as can be seen from the letter to the Galatians, the question as to which of the Old Testament rules still applied continued to be a problem for some.

The sacrifices were fulfilled at the Cross of Christ and so clearly no long apply. But the foundation of the moral laws was laid before the Law of Moses was given. This certainly applies, as already noted, to the question of marriage and sex. Such laws are still needed if God's creation is to function properly.

Sex and Adultery

The seventh commandment is upheld in the New Testament. When Jesus was asked what must be done to inherit eternal life, His initial reply was, "You know the commandments: 'Do not commit adultery ...'" (Luke 18:18-20). The writer of Hebrews says that God will judge the adulterous (Hebrews 13:4). The message of the Lord to the church in Thyatira was that He would bring those who were committing adultery with the woman Jezebel into "great tribulation" unless they repented (Revelation 2:22).

The New Testament standard is higher than that of the Old Testament. Jesus said that to look on a woman with "lustful intent" was to commit adultery with her in the heart (Matthew 5:27-30). Adultery is one of those things that defile because it comes from the heart (Matthew 7:21).

Under Old Testament standards a man could have sex with an unattached woman and it would not have been counted as adultery. But in Hebrews 13:4 it refers to those who are "sexually immoral and adulterous". The word for "sexually immoral" could be translated as "fornicators". The word refers to sex outside of marriage and is something from which the Christian must abstain (1 Thessalonians 4:3-8). If they do not abstain they will be "wronging their brother". That is, when those who have engaged in unmarried sex eventually come to marry someone they will not be coming to the marriage as virgins. Their spouses will be wronged in that they will be "second-hand goods". According to Hebrews 13:4, everyone, whether married or single must hold marriage in honour. Every Christian must exercise self-control

(1 Thessalonians 4:4); this they have available since it is part of the fruit of the Spirit (Galatians 5:22-23).

Old Testament laws about divorce are recorded in Deuteronomy 24:1-4. The law is to ensure that a divorced woman who remarries, if she is divorced again, may not return to her first husband. It came to be applied as permission to divorce. As Jesus said, that was not God's intention at the beginning. There it is said that a man shall "hold fast to his wife, and they shall become one flesh" (Genesis 2:24). The only grounds for divorce that Jesus allows is when the oneness of the marriage has been broken by "sexual immorality" (Matthew 19:9). Remarriage after divorce on any other grounds constitutes adultery. These rules on divorce apply equally to women who divorce their husbands (Mark 10:11-12).

Homosexual Practice

It is clear that as far as the New Testament writers are concerned the practice of homosexuality is ungodly. Paul writes about men being "consumed with passion for one another" (Romans 1:27), and he says that this is the result of "exchanging the truth of God for a lie" (Romans 1:25). When writing to the church at Corinth Paul reminds them that before they came to know Christ some of them were men who practised homosexuality (1 Corinthians 6:9-11). But when they came to Christ they were made clean, forgiven and set apart to live lives pleasing to God.

Lesbian behaviour is not mentioned in Leviticus 18, probably because it was neither a current practice nor envisaged. But Paul writes of women exchanging natural relations for the unnatural as another result of rejecting the truth about God (Romans 1:26).

Children

The worship of Molech had long since died out by New Testament times. However, in Jewish society, a child was thought to be of no importance. A child was a responsibility, someone to be looked after. They were regarded as nonentities. But Jesus set them up as examples. Unless a person becomes like a child, realising how undeserving they are in the sight of God and in need of his grace, they will never enter God's kingdom (Matthew18:2-3). So Jesus welcomed children and blessed them saying that the kingdom of God belongs to nonentities (Matthew 19:13-15). Christian parents must also value their children (Ephesians 6:4; Colossians 3:21).

Abundant Life

Jesus said that He had come to give abundant life to His sheep, that is, to those who follow Him (John 10:10). Following Jesus, obeying God's laws, results in nothing but good.

If God's laws were accepted, people would see themselves as the crown of God's creation, not as animals. It would be recognised that, although sex is meant to be enjoyed, it is intended for procreation not simply to gratify lust. As a result, women would be treated with respect rather than as sex objects.

Relationships would be valued. A husband would be faithful to his wife and a wife to her husband. Parents would value their children and treat them as God's gifts, bringing them up in God's ways and lovingly disciplining them with great care (Ephesians 6:4; Colossians 3:21). The harm that children of broken families suffer would be eliminated.

Following Jesus would have an impact on the environment. For one thing, if the whole world followed him, sexually transmitted diseases would come to an end.

Through their disobedience, Adam and Eve brought death into the world (Genesis 2:17) and were banished from access to the tree of life (Genesis 3:22-23). Through His obedience, Jesus has brought the tree of life into the centre of the New Jerusalem, the Church. That life is available for all to enjoy – the leaves of the tree of life are "for the healing of the nations" (Revelation 22:1-2). In all that God has done and continues to do, His purpose is to restore abundant life to His creation.

Life in Society
Leviticus 19

Important to Christians?

The problem with understanding some parts of the Bible is knowing what to take literally, which commands should be obeyed exactly. It is obvious that Christians are not expected to obey the commands relating to the sacrifices since they have been fulfilled in Christ. But with some of the rules in Leviticus 19 the answer is not so obvious. We no longer need to be reminded about the rules for eating the peace offering (5-8), but is it alright for a Christian to wear clothing made of a mixture of polyester and cotton? (19).

Some of the commands of Leviticus 19 are reiterated or approved in the New Testament. God tells his people that they must imitate him (2). Peter quotes that verse (1 Peter 1:16) and Jesus gave the same command to his disciples (Matthew 5:48). Jesus said that loving one's neighbour as oneself (18) is one of the two commandments on which "all the Law and the Prophets depend" (Matthew 22:37-40) and James calls that command "the royal law" (James 2:8). James also refers to verse 15 of this chapter when he says that dishonouring a poor man in favour of the rich is breaking the law (James 2:1-9). So Jesus and the New Testament writers find a basis in Leviticus 19 for what they have to say about the way we treat one another.

The Old Testament moral law deals with principles rather than details. In their commentaries the rabbis tried to explain the moral law in great detail, for example by stating what constituted work on the Sabbath. But all they succeeded in doing was to "load people with burdens hard to bear" (Luke 11:46). The moral law of the Old Testament states principles which the God-fearing person learns to apply in each situation.

The Starting Point

The basic principle that God gives for life in society is right at the centre of this chapter: "You shall love your neighbour as yourself" (18). But simply setting out to obey that command does not guarantee success. The starting point is God Himself.

The chapter begins with the call to imitate God, to be holy because He is holy (2). Keeping separate what God has created separate (19) is a symbol of holiness.

105

It continues with a reminder that the foundation for a Godly society is Godly families and they are achieved when children revere their parents (3). The word for revere is the same as that used in verses 14 & 32 ("fear") of a right attitude to God. In the family, parents are to behave as God's earthly representatives and are to be revered as such.

Observing the Sabbath (3, 30) is a reminder and an acknowledgement that God made everything and that, therefore, everything belongs to Him. They are to reverence God's sanctuary (30) since it is there that God's presence dwells.

They are not to turn to idols or make them (4), but they must remain faithful to their God. The reminder about not consuming blood (26) probably relates to a pagan ritual since it is followed immediately by a ban on interpreting omens and telling fortunes. The prohibitions of 27-28 relate to a pagan cult of the dead. The warning against mediums and necromancers (31) refers to Canaanite ancestor worship. So throughout the chapter God repeatedly reminds them of the vital importance of remaining faithful to Him.

All of this is hammered home by the statement, "I am the LORD", which God makes fifteen times in this chapter. In seven of those the words "your God" are added. The chapter ends with a call to obey all God's laws because "I am the LORD". The starting point, and the reason for persevering in loving one's neighbour is God, His holiness, what He has done for them, and the fact that He is their God and they are His people.

So there are reminders throughout the chapter that the commandment to love your neighbour as yourself does not stand alone. It stands with and follows from the commandment to love the LORD your God with all your heart, soul, mind and strength (Matthew 22:37-40).

The Royal Law

It is clear from the immediate context of verse 18 that loving one's neighbour is not about feelings but about actions and thoughts. God's people are not to take vengeance or to bear grudges (18). In fact the whole chapter is about actions.

This is confirmed in the New Testament. Jesus said, "Whatever you wish that others would do to you, do also to them, for this is the Law and the Prophets" (Matthew 7:12). Paul wrote, "Let no one seek his own good, but the good of his neighbour" (1 Corinthians 10:24). Both these statements show that loving one's neighbour is not a matter of paying someone back for the good

106

they have done, but setting out to do good whatever they have or have not done.

Leviticus 19 also shows that the concept of neighbour is not confined to friends and close acquaintances but also includes the foreigner who is living with God's people (33-34). Jesus broadened the definition of neighbour to include one's enemy in His parable of the Good Samaritan (Luke 10:25-37).

The chapter sets out guiding principles for loving one's neighbour. They are set out in a very random way, but it may help to think of them under five headings: Generosity, Honesty, Kindness, Respect and Justice.

Generosity

The whole animal for a peace offering (5-8) was brought to God (3:1). The fat, the kidneys and the liver were burnt on the altar, but God gave the rest of the meat back to be eaten. It was a gift from God and eaten in God's presence as host. God was to be shown great respect in that the meat was to be eaten by the second day, before it began to decay. When it came to food, God was to come first, but He was generous in giving to His people.

Once that was established instructions could be given about food for the poor (9-10). Leaving some of the crop unharvested provided food for those who had little or no land of their own. Gleaning was hard work but this gave the poor a measure of dignity which handouts would not have done. For the farmer it served as a reminder that everything good comes from God, so the crop was not his to do with as he liked. It put the brake on greed and made the farmer trust God for the future instead of filling his barns while others went hungry.

The meaning of the instructions about fruit trees (23-25) is not clear. Agriculturalists say that to leave the fruit on the tree for three years would not result in an increased yield in the fifth year. They say that if verse 23 means that the buds were to be picked out before the fruit had formed, this would have resulted in an improved yield. Whatever the details, if the instructions were followed it would result in putting God first (24), trusting God for the future and providing for posterity (25), rather than living for oneself for the present. So love for God and for others is at the heart of these rules.

Jesus encouraged his disciples to give (Luke 6:38). The kind of practical love of which God spoke in Leviticus 19 was practised by the early church (2 Corinthians 8).

Food banks have become necessary in some parts of England and they meet the immediate needs of some. But they are handouts. The modern equivalent of Leviticus is the kind of organization which provides the funds to set people up in small businesses. This provides them with an income and with the sense of dignity that working for one's living gives.

Honesty

Imagine that a man steals a sheep, or sells a cow for more than it is worth (11). When he is confronted with his crime he denies it. The wronged man persists in his accusations and gathers the elders of the village as witnesses. The wrongdoer, desperate to escape punishment, swears by the LORD that he is not guilty (12). To stealing or crooked dealing he has added lying and then, worst of all, he has profaned God's name (12). God's name represents the whole of his being. The wrongdoer has brought God in on his side and so associated God with dishonesty, thus injuring God's reputation. He has broken the third commandment (Exodus 20:7) in which God had said that taking His name in vain would be punished.

In the words of Sir Walter Scott, "Oh what a tangled web we weave when first we practise to deceive."

Honesty was to be practised in the marketplace (35-36). Integrity there was to be total, whether measuring length, weight or quantity. This was so important that the rule is expressed both as a prohibition (35) and as a command (36). In the last part of verse 36 God was telling them that if they did not obey Him in this, they would be as bad as the Egyptians.

Imagine a society in which there was no stealing, cheating or lying. There would be less of a need for police or members of the legal profession. People would be at ease knowing they could trust one another. That society would be one of trust and peace.

Paul had to appeal to the Christians at Ephesus, "let each one of you speak the truth with his neighbour, for we are members one of another". He even found it necessary to say "let the thief no longer steal" (Ephesians 4:25 & 28). He was shocked to hear that the Christians in Corinth were defrauding one another (1 Corinthians 6:8).

A church cannot function properly, and will bring dishonour on the name of Christ, if its members are not honest with one another.

Kindness

The thought behind the command not to oppress one's neighbour (13) is that of taking advantage of someone who is weaker or dependent. An employee was particularly vulnerable because his employer could withhold his wages if he did not, for example, work extra hours. This is probably why, in a chapter about rules for society, God twice repeats the command to keep His Sabbaths (3, 30). By speaking of "my Sabbaths" God makes it clear that it is not only the seventh day that He has in mind. He is commanding that every employee must be free to enjoy every one of God's "holidays".

A society that is driven by a desire to create wealth without interruption will not be a healthy society. When wealth is the most important thing it gives rise to other problems. "The love of money is a root of all kinds of evil" (1 Timothy 6:10). People need to be able to stop and remind themselves that riches are unreliable (1 Timothy 6:17); that it is only treasure in heaven that lasts (Matthew 6:20); that godliness with contentment yields the best profit (1 Timothy 6:6); that everything good is from God (James 1:17).

An employer was to pay fair wages, he was not to "rob" his employee (13). The worker was to be paid daily, which was the norm. This enabled him, for example, to buy the "daily bread" (Matthew 6:11) for himself and his family. Delaying payment would result in hunger and hardship. So the employer was to pay wages on time (13), however inconvenient that might be for him.

James warns rich people that their riches will not last (James 1:10). He says that God knows when they withhold due wages and he hears the cries of those who are being wronged (James 5:4). He refers to God as "the Lord of hosts": He is the one who dealt with wrong in Old Testament times and who is still able to do so, and will do so again. So James encourages Christians who are being defrauded, and who have no legal means of redress, to "be patient … until the coming of the Lord" (James 5:7).

Respect

The foundation for a respectful attitude towards others is laid in the family. As already noted, parents are to act as God's representatives and children are to revere them as such. Children who have not been brought up to respect their parents are the cause of major problems for teachers today. Such children have no respect for one another, let alone their teachers.

The disabled must be treated with respect (14). It can be amusing to say something derogatory about a deaf person while knowing that they cannot hear what is said. It may raise a laugh to see a blind person trip over an obstacle placed in their way. But the disabled are made in God's image, and to take advantage in any way of any disablement is an offence against their Maker. The ultimate deterrent against such behaviour is to have a proper fear of God (14) who will vindicate His weak people (Deuteronomy 32:36).

The punishment due to a man who has sex with his female slave when she has been assigned to another (20-22) seems very lenient. If both man and woman had been free, they would both have been stoned to death (Deuteronomy 22:23-24), but in this case "a distinction shall be made … because she was not free". The man has not yet received the ransom price so he still owns her. Nothing illegal has been done, but the man has failed to show respect for both the woman and her future husband. He has trespassed on their rights and must bring a guilt offering to the LORD (22). This illustrates how important to God it is that property rights be respected even when it is an "engagement" and the "marriage" has yet to take place.

Parents must treat their children with respect. There have been many times in many cultures where the struggle to survive has been so desperate that parents have sold their children into prostitution. Parents who do this to a daughter are degrading her and the ultimate result will be that others will follow the practice and the whole nation will fall into prostitution (29). New Testament instructions are that while children are to respect their parents by obeying them, parents are to respect their children by not provoking or exasperating them (Ephesians 6:1-4).

It may no longer be necessary to actually stand up when an elderly person enters a room (32). But in Isaiah we see that lack of respect for the elderly is a sign of a failing society. God says that when He removes His support from Judah (Isaiah 3:1), one of the results will be that "the youth will be insolent to the elder", and He parallels this with despised people being insolent to those who are honourable (Isaiah 3:5). The elderly should be honoured for the experience and wisdom they have gained through their long lives. It should be noted that, as with having respect for the disabled (14), this rule is also supported by the command to fear God (32).

Justice

In Old Testament times courts were convened only when there was a problem to be resolved. There were no special buildings and the judges were the local elders. The communities were small and everybody knew each other. The elders would know both the accused and the plaintive and one or the other might be a particular friend of one or more of the elders. So the temptation to be "partial to the poor" or to "defer to the great" (15) was a real possibility. Judgements had to be made "in righteousness", that is, in ways which would be God-pleasing and would ensure the well-being of the community.

Members of the community had to be careful not to unduly influence the decision of the court. People would have had their own opinions about the rights and wrongs of the matter and would have been inclined to go around gossiping (16). The community being small, the elders would have heard what was being said and could have been moved to pre-judge the case before hearing the evidence. People were to be especially careful in cases where guilt incurred the death penalty (16).

When bringing a matter before the elders care had to be taken that the motive for doing so was not personal hatred (17). This might have arisen because of something that had been done long before, resulting in a grudge and a desire for revenge (18). The better way was to "reason frankly" with each other (17). If the two parties could get together and calmly talk things through, there might be no need to go to court.

Paul was evidently shocked to hear that the Christians in Corinth were taking each other to court (1 Corinthians 6:1-7). He tells them that they ought to be able to settle matters among themselves. It was better to simply put up with being wronged than to parade their differences before non-Christians.

He tells the Christians in Rome to leave vengeance to God since that is his prerogative (Deuteronomy 32:35). Instead they are to care for an enemy, for example by giving him food and drink. By returning good for evil they would "heap burning coals on his head", that is, they would bring about a drastic change of mind in their enemy (Romans 12:19-20).

"A soft answer turns away wrath, but a harsh word stirs up anger." (Proverbs 15:1)

The Lord Jesus told his disciples not to take legal action even though that might mean suffering further wrong (Matthew 5:39). If on the other hand they are taken to court, rather than fight the case, they should give more than is being asked (Matthew 5:40). This was contrary to the contemporary attitude of "an eye for an eye".

Tit for tat retaliation can escalate into war unless someone is willing to say that enough is enough.

Practical Holiness

Love for God and love for one's neighbour are inseparable. An absence of the former will result in the love of self and the welfare of a neighbour will not even be considered. Love for God that involves all the heart, soul, mind and strength will result in regarding the needs of a neighbour as at least as important as one's own.

The rules expressed in Leviticus 19 for loving one's neighbour are relevant to Christians today. Applying them would transform our society. But, since love for God is the first essential, and since such love cannot be imposed by law, the only hope we have of changing our self-absorbed society is to proclaim the truth and show by our lives that it works.

Punishment
Leviticus 20

Crimes and Consequences

The subjects of this chapter are the same as those of chapter 18: worship of Molech, adultery, incest, homosexuality, bestiality and sexual intercourse during menstruation. It also deals with two subjects of chapter 19: cursing parents and consulting mediums and necromancers. The difference is that, whereas chapters 18 and 19 simply prohibit these sins, chapter 20 details the punishments that are due to those who offend.

The punishments

In this chapter the death penalty is stipulated for worshipping Molech (2) or cursing parents (9), for committing adultery (10) or incest (11, 12, 14), for practising homosexuality (13) or bestiality (15, 16), and for those who call up or consult the dead (27). The method of execution is specified in verse 2 but not elsewhere. Execution was usually carried out by throwing the offender off a cliff, and then stoning if the fall did not prove fatal. This was considered to be the most humane form of execution. It also had the advantage of being carried out by the community rather than by an individual appointed as executioner. In the case of a man having both a woman and her mother as his wives (14), burning is specified, but this would have been done after they had been executed.

God told Moses that in certain cases the offenders would be "cut off". It is clear from verse 3 that this was something that God would do. In those days there was no police force. It was up to those who had been wronged, or had seen or heard an offence committed, to take the offender before the elders and so commence the process of justice. But some of these offences could be committed in secret, so there would be no public exposure and no trial. However, God would ensure that justice was done, and done in such a way that everyone would know: they would be "cut off in the sight of the children of their people" (17).

Being cut off could mean immediate or premature death, or the family line being brought to an end, perhaps by children pre-deceasing their parents. Being cut off was to be the fate of those who knew that a couple had given their first-born to Molech but had failed to make it known to the elders (4, 5). It was also to be the fate of those who consulted mediums and necromancers

(6). It was to be the penalty for incest with a sister or half-sister (17), or for having sex with a woman who was menstruating (18).

Childlessness is predicted for two offences (19-21). This may refer to a particular aspect of being cut off. Children were valued as a sign of God's blessing and to be deprived of them a sign of God's displeasure.

Those who gave their children to Molech would suffer both the death penalty (2) and being cut off by God (3). Perhaps this double punishment was because of the double offence – idolatry and murder.

Reasonable Demands

In our 21st century society in which the guiding principle for most people is to stay alive for as long as possible whatever the cost, these rules seem harsh and brutal. But they would have seemed reasonable to the Israelites. God had rescued them from slavery in Egypt where they had suffered the brutality which was the common lot of slaves. He had kept them alive in the wilderness by providing manna and quails. They owed Him a great deal. Furthermore, if by obeying God's laws they could avoid the loss of life which the Canaanites would suffer through their wickedness (23), they would have been glad to do so. What they eventually suffered at the hands of their enemies, in particular the Assyrians and Babylonians, demonstrated how right they had been to obey and how foolish to fall into disobedience.

Humanitarian Emphases

The laws in this chapter have to do with people - wrongs done to people or wrongs that people do to themselves (15-16). It is on such crimes that God imposes the greatest penalties.

Crimes against property were more leniently dealt with in that only restitution was required. For example, if a man stole an animal, he had to repay five oxen for a stolen ox or four sheep for a stolen sheep (Exodus 22:1). By contrast, in Mesopotamia the punishment for theft was death, and a long and painful death at that.

In Mesopotamia being forgiven and restored to society was not an option for a thief. But it is obvious from the laws for the guilt offering (5:14-6:7) that God desired and offered forgiveness and restoration for those who offended against property. Once restitution had been made to the one who had been wronged, and to God by means of a guilt offering, the offender was received back into society. Atonement had been made and the matter was closed.

In the same spirit, an offender was not to be humiliated. The severity of a punishment was limited. For example, if a man deserved to be beaten, the number of strokes was not to exceed forty lest "your brother be degraded in your sight" (Deuteronomy 25:1-3).

So God places a greater value on people than He does on things.

The Purposes of Punishment

It was not the purpose of the justice system in Israel to give opportunities for revenge (19:18). Vengeance was and is God's prerogative (Deuteronomy 32:35).

God's purposes in imposing punishment on offenders are made clear in Deuteronomy 19:19-21. These verses show that punishment was intended to ensure that the offender received what he legally deserved (verse 19a). So it was to be "eye for eye, tooth for tooth" (verse 21) – the punishment must fit the crime and not be excessive. God also wanted to ensure that evil behaviour by an individual was stopped before the whole society was infected (verse 19b). The punishment would also serve as a deterrent (verse 20). It was right that the one who had been wronged should receive compensation (verse 21). Deterrent and compensation were achieved, for example, by the thief having to pay back four or five times what he had stolen (Exodus 22:1).

The death penalty

The method of execution used by the Israelites was considered to be the most humane. This was in contrast to the methods used by the surrounding nations. For example, in Esther 5:14, later than the time of Leviticus but typical, Haman is advised to get his revenge on Mordecai by making a "gallows" and "hanging" Mordecai on it. The words may conjure up a picture of a gibbet and a rope with a noose, but the hanging meant impaling on a sharpened pole pushed up through the intestines. The death inflicted was slow and agonising; the victim was degraded by being on display for a matter of days. In Israel the matter was over very quickly. There was no waiting on death row, death was close to instantaneous, and the dying or dead were not on display to shame and degrade the victim and his family.

Another distinctive and humane feature of God's law was in the matter of who was to be executed. In Assyria, if a building collapsed and the son of the house was killed, the guilty builder could have his son executed in his place.

God's law for Israel was that the guilty one should die for his own sin (Deuteronomy 24:16).

It is reckoned that there were seventeen offences in the Old Testament law for which the penalty was death. These included murder (Exodus 21:12), kidnapping (Exodus 21:16), cursing one's parents (Exodus 21:17), failing to keep a dangerous animal in check (Exodus 21:29), false prophecy (Deuteronomy 13:1-5), breaking the Sabbath (Exodus 31:14-15), blasphemy (Leviticus 24:16) and idolatry (Deuteronomy 13:6-9). But there are reasons for thinking that the death penalty was probably not carried out as frequently as the long list might suggest.

For one thing, the death sentence would not have been passed without due process; there had to be at least two witnesses whose testimony agreed (Deuteronomy 17:6). Then it seems that the payment of a ransom could have rescued a condemned person from death. God told Moses that a murderer must be put to death; he could not be rescued by the payment of a ransom (Numbers 35:31). This specific prohibition suggests that for other crimes a ransom would have been acceptable.

The New Testament and the Death Penalty

Capital punishment for murder was abolished in the UK in 1965 and completely abolished in 1998. But in the USA it is still legal in thirty-two of the fifty states. Christian opinion on the subject is divided in the USA, with some holding that the Bible, in particular Leviticus 20, supports the use of execution as a punishment for certain crimes, especially for murder.

The teaching of the Lord Jesus does not give any clear direction on this matter. He appears to criticise the Pharisees for not enforcing the law about cursing one's parents (Matthew 15:1-6), but told the woman caught in the act of adultery that He didn't condemn her but to "sin no more" (John 8:1-11).

Paul wrote a list of offences including murder, hating God and being disobedient to parents and refers to "God's righteous decree that those who practise such things deserve to die" (Romans 1:29-32). But since much of the list is made up of character traits, it is probable that Paul is referring to God's decree stated at the beginning (Genesis 2:17) rather than to the Law of Moses.

It is clear that the ritual laws have been fulfilled in Christ and that the moral law is still upheld in the New Testament. But the Sabbath-breaking law, for example, is neither ritual nor moral. Under the Old Testament law it was punishable by death. Does that still apply today?

It seems that the early church met on the first day of the week (Acts 20:7; 1 Corinthians 16:2) rather than the seventh. Many Christians would have been obliged to work for their masters on both the seventh day and the first, but there is no word of condemnation for that. The letter written to Gentile Christians at the conclusion of the Council of Jerusalem makes no reference to observing the Sabbath (Acts 15:27-29). Indeed, Paul appeals to Christians in Rome to be tolerant of those who have different opinions about the relative importance of different days (Romans 14:5-6).

If the death penalty is no longer applicable to Sabbath-breaking, a straight transfer of Old Testament punishments to the offences of today would be to over-simplify the problem.

There is no clear teaching given in the New Testament on the rights or wrongs of capital punishment.

Influencing Societies

At the time of the giving of the Law Israel was a theocracy, God giving instructions directly to Moses.

The Israel of Moses' day was of a single culture and of one religion, and the aspiration of the majority was to please God by obeying His laws. In that context it would be expected that anyone who departed from God's ways would be punished, especially when the whole nation might suffer the consequences of the disobedience. But Israel was not commanded to impose its laws on other nations. God's people were to obey God's laws and, by so doing, stand out in sharp contrast to the ungodliness and brutality of their neighbours.

Britain is a secular society in which laws are agreed by a process of democracy. It is a society of many cultures and religions, all with different opinions about acceptable behaviour. The majority of the population do not accept the authority of the God of the Bible. So what influence on society should the Church and individual Christians expect to have?

Christ did not send the apostles into the world to impose God's laws on others. He sent them to make disciples, to teach people to observe all that He had commanded (Matthew 28:18-20). The aim of their preaching and teaching was that individuals would accept Christ and be born again of the Spirit of

God. When that happened they would enter God's kingdom (John 3:5) and so submit themselves to God's will. So the prime task of the Church is to preach and teach the Gospel and pray that the Holy Spirit will use the Word to draw others to Christ.

Should Christians aim to have any influence on governments, the laws they pass and the way those laws are administered?

Paul says that Christians should be subject to the ruling powers because those powers receive their authority from God. The one in authority is God's servant and has the good of every one of his subjects at heart. The fact that "he bears the sword" is included among his duties as God's servant (Romans 13:1-7). However, in Revelation 13, written not more than 40 years later, the power of Rome is depicted as a beast that receives its authority from the dragon, the Devil.

So every generation has to decide where on the spectrum between Romans 13 and Revelation 13 the government of the day stands, and where on that same spectrum individual laws, proposed or passed by that government, stand. Christians in Britain should take advantage of their democratic rights to support or oppose governments and laws in accordance with the revealed will of God. In the past 30 or 40 years there have been opportunities to argue that God's ways are best in matters such as Sunday trading, abortion, euthanasia and marriage.

A Call to Holiness

This chapter delivers another call from God to His people to be holy (7, 26). In order to be holy the Israelites had to guard all God's laws and commandments and put them into practice (8, 22). They had to make sure that they were not influenced by the practices of the surrounding nations and enticed into their ways (23-24). God had separated them from all other nations (24-26) and they were to maintain that separation in religion and behaviour. Verse 25 is an illustration of what it meant to maintain the distinction between what is acceptable to God and what is not. It is a reminder that holiness is not just a spiritual matter but affects every aspect of life.

It was vital that Israel remained holy, retained that separation, because the consequences of sin, of disobeying God's laws were serious. Some of the immediate costs are obvious: first-born sons given to Molech and a mother's anguish; incest and adultery destroying families; jealousy and suspicion because no-one can trust anyone else; society falling apart.

More seriously, failure to be holy would result in separation from God. It would result in having God as their enemy as He had become the enemy of the Canaanites (23). God would set His face against them and cut them off (3, 5, and 6). It would be of no use trying to shift the blame onto something or someone else. The individual was to be held responsible for his own sin (3), and the community that condoned sin was held responsible for that (4-5). If the nation persisted in sinning and condoning sin then eventually God's creation would revolt and they would be vomited out of the land (22), and God wanted them to enjoy the "land flowing with milk and honey" (24).

Becoming and remaining holy is not easy. It required them to make a conscious decision and a determined effort to set themselves apart for God (7a). But it was not all down to them. God, the LORD, who had set them apart to be His people (26), was continuing to set them apart (8b) by giving them His laws. He would go on calling His people to holiness by reminding them of His laws through Godly leaders and faithful prophets.

A Lesson for Today

The foundation upon which God based His appeal to Israel to be holy was the closeness of their relationship with Him. He was "the LORD" (7) who had rescued them from Egypt so He was their God (7) and they belonged to Him (26).

Two of the metaphors used in the New Testament to explain the relationship between the Church and Christ particularly emphasise how close that relationship is.

Paul writes about the Church being the body of Christ (1 Corinthians 12:27). This is not just a corporate relationship because he goes on to say to the Corinthian Christians that they are "individually members" of Christ's body. In the same letter he points out how inappropriate it would be for a member of Christ's body to have relations with a prostitute (1 Corinthians 6:15-16).

The other metaphor is that of wife and husband. In his letter to the church at Ephesus Paul quotes the verse from Genesis 2, "Therefore a man shall leave his father and mother and hold fast to his wife, and the two shall become one flesh." He goes on to say that this ultimately refers to "Christ and the Church" (Ephesians 5:31-32). Paul wrote to the church in Corinth, "I betrothed you to one husband, to present you as a pure virgin to Christ" (2 Corinthians 11:2).

Cursing parents (Matthew 15:4), the practice of homosexuality (Romans 1:18-32) and sexual immorality (1 Corinthians 5:1-5) are still treated as serious in the New Testament. The closeness of the relationship between Christ and the Church is such that it makes all aspects of ungodliness totally inappropriate. Whatever else in this chapter may be open to debate, it is clear that the call to be holy is something that Christians can and should apply to themselves (1 Peter 1:15-16).

Leaders and Followers
Leviticus 21 and 22
Leaders' Responsibilities

Leaders who are not simply self-appointed but recognised and accepted as leaders, will have a following. So they have to be careful what steps they take, what paths they follow, because they will take others along with them. Spiritual leaders have a special responsibility to avoid being associated with what is wrong or giving the impression that they approve of wrong-doing.

There was an extra factor for the spiritual leaders of the Old Testament, shown in 21:6. The priests "offer the LORD's food offerings, the bread of their God". For a priest to perform the rituals of the sanctuary while unclean or in any way unfit to do so would be like a servant presenting food to his master with filthy hands and clothes. That would be an insult to his master. A priest entering the sanctuary and performing the rituals in a manner or in a condition that was in any sense unholy, would profane God's name (21:6). He would damage God's reputation and soil God's sanctuary (21:23).

Appropriate Mourning

Just as touching the carcass of an animal rendered a person unclean (11:39), so did touching a corpse or being in the same room as a dead body. Even though the purification rites were faithfully observed, the uncleanness would last seven days (Numbers 19:11-14). Attending a funeral would mean coming into close proximity with the dead even if the body itself was not touched. For a priest this would mean that he would be unable to perform his duties for a week. The service of God must come first, so the priest must avoid taking part in funeral rites. However, God understands the sorrow caused by the death of a loved one (John 11:35), and the priest was allowed to join in the ceremonies for his mother, father, son, daughter, brother or unmarried sister (21:2-3). But he was forbidden from taking part in the funerals of in-laws (21:4).

Since a priest and his wife would be "one flesh", it is almost certain that, normally, he would have been permitted to take part in mourning for his wife and in the funeral rites. This is borne out by the fact that Ezekiel, who was a priest (Ezekiel 1:3), was specifically commanded not to weep or to show any signs of mourning for his dead wife (Ezekiel 24:15-18).

In this country it has been customary to wear black while in mourning. In Old Testament times tearing one's clothes and wearing rough cloth next to the skin was common practice (Genesis 37:34). When Israel's neighbours mourned they disfigured themselves in one way or another, by shaving parts of their hair or beards or by cutting themselves (21:5). Such actions were particularly associated with the worship of the dead. This was forbidden to the priest who must not in any way show approval of pagan practices. To do so might encourage the people to take a first step towards the worship of pagan gods.

For the chief priest the requirements were much stricter (21:10-12). He must not show any signs of mourning at all. At his ordination his hair had been anointed; his special clothes were made to set him apart as chief priest. So to disarrange his hair or tear his clothes would have symbolised a cancellation of his priesthood. The service of God must come first. Even for the funeral of his mother or father he must not leave the sanctuary.

Acceptable Marriage

A priest was not permitted to marry a prostitute (21:7) because her history of sexual behaviour was very evidently ungodly, and marrying her would give tacit approval to such behaviour. This was especially important since most prostitution was associated with the worship of fertility gods. Neither must he marry any woman whose history of sexual behaviour was in any doubt. The ex-husband of a divorced woman may have had good reason to send her away. So for a priest to marry any woman who had been "defiled" (21:7) would bring the priesthood into disrepute and could set the wrong example. Perhaps the purpose of verse 8 is to ensure that, in those days of arranged marriages, no pressure was put on a priest to marry a woman who was not suitable.

The seriousness of a priest being associated with sexual immorality is further emphasised by the command that, if his daughter turned to prostitution she must be burnt (21:9).

Once again the standard for the chief priest was higher. It seems from verse 14 that a priest was permitted to marry a widow. But the chief priest had to marry a virgin (21:13, 14). She had to be "of his own people", so that she would be well-known and there would be no doubt about her virginity. Marrying a virgin would ensure that there could be no question about the paternity of their children (21:15). This was important because the office of chief priest was hereditary; his son would be anointed, wear the special robes and enter the Most Holy Place on the Day of Atonement. An imposter could not properly represent the people before God and if he entered the Most Holy Place he would die.

Physical Qualifications

A descendant of Aaron who had "a blemish" (21:17) was not permitted to offer sacrifices or enter the Holy Place (21:17, 23). A list of blemishes is given in verses 18-20, but this is probably intended to illustrate the kind of defect that applied, rather than to provide a complete catalogue.

The reason for this rule is that, especially in the Old Testament, the physical is symbolic of and illustrative of the spiritual. The body represents the whole person; an imperfect body indicates an imperfect person. Holiness was symbolised by normality. This was the case in the definitions of clean and unclean animals (Leviticus 11). So an abnormal body symbolised an unholy person. For a man with a blemished body to enter the sanctuary would be like announcing that unholiness was acceptable to God.

It was not that the man himself was evil or that he was rejected by God. He was allowed to share the food that was the priests' due from the offerings (21:22), even what was "most holy". This included what remained from the offerings (2:10; 6:29; 7:6). So, even though because of his blemishes he could not officiate as a priest, God made sure that he was provided for. God valued him as a person and preserved his dignity.

Respectful Eating

The priests had to be careful that familiarity with the sacrificial system did not breed contempt. They must treat the sacrifices presented by the people with respect (22:2 NIV). Being careless in these things would bring dishonour to God's name (22:2) and they would die (22:9). This applied to the eating of the meat from those sacrifices.

Priests were not due any special privileges. If a priest was unclean for any of the reasons given for lay people in chapters 13-15 he was forbidden from offering sacrifices on pain of death (22:3). He was also prohibited from eating of the meat from the sacrifices (22:4-9). He was subject to the same rules for cleansing as the lay person, that is, he would be unclean for the rest of the day and then he had to wash himself (22:6). When those rites had been observed he could eat of the food.

The priests had to show respect for the offerings by being careful that only those with the God-given right to eat of them did so. Only the priests and those who were dependent on them for their food qualified. Foreign guests had their own sources of income and hired workers received their wages so they were not permitted to eat (22:10). But slaves who had been purchased, and all those born in the priest's household were true dependents and would share the food (22:11). When the daughter of a priest married she became the responsibility of her husband (22:12). If she returned to her father's home as a childless widow or divorcee she would become her father's responsibility once again (22:13). If she had children it would be their responsibility to care for their mother, assuming they were capable of doing so.

In this matter of the eating of food from the sacrifices, offences committed unintentionally had to be atoned for. If, for example, a guest or a hired worker ate of the priest's food not realising that it was forbidden, that was no excuse and a guilt offering would be due (22:14-16; 5:14-16).

Disrespectful Offerings

The blemishes that make an animal unacceptable for sacrifice were the same as those that disqualified a descendant of Aaron from performing the duties of a priest. The reason was the same: abnormal means unclean and unclean equals unholy.

The stipulation that a sacrificial animal must be without blemish was repeated for every one of the sacrifices. In this chapter details are given (22:20-25). The list is intended to illustrate the kind of defect that applied, rather than to provide a complete catalogue of blemishes. The instructions are given in detail here because it was the priest's responsibility to make a decision and to reject any animal that was unacceptable. He must not make any exceptions, not even for relatives or friends. The animals were being given "to the LORD" (22:18, 21, 22, 24). He would not accept what was imperfect, and so it would not be "accepted for you" (22:19, 20, 25); it would not be effective in making atonement or as a peace offering. The only exception to this was if the peace offering was a freewill offering. In that case a bull or a lamb that had "a part too long or too short" would be accepted (22:23).

Quality not Quantity

There are occasions recorded in the Old Testament when so many animals were killed in sacrifice that one wonders what it was like with so much blood being poured out (e.g. 1 Kings 8:5). But the laws of Leviticus show that it is not the quantity of sacrifices that pleases God. What would please Him would be giving the kind of sacrifices that He required, and giving them in the way that He had laid down.

A number of regulations were given in the Law which restricted bloodshed. Leviticus 11 limited the varieties of animal which could be eaten. Leviticus 17 required that if a domestic animal were killed it must be brought to the entrance of the Tent of Meeting, and that when an animal was killed in the hunt its blood must be disposed of in a particular way. If a nest were found containing a mother bird with eggs or young, the eggs or young could be taken but the mother bird had to be left (Deuteronomy 22:6).

These restrictions were not only what might be called religious, they also served to protect the environment.

The rules of 22:27-28 provide more details of how avoiding unnecessary bloodshed might work out in practice. They emphasise that it was not a matter of the greater the number of animals sacrificed, the better God would be pleased. What was important was that the right animal should be brought, offered for the right reason and sacrificed in the right way. The repetition of the rules for eating the meat from a sacrifice (22:29-30) stresses the need to do things in the right way.

Motivation

Six times in these two chapters God says that He is the one who sanctifies, the one who makes things holy. He does this to and for the people (21:8; 22:32), the chief priest (21:15), the sanctuary (21:23) and the priests (22:9, 16). This has two sides to it. First it is a warning that what God has made holy should be treated as holy by God's people. This is particularly obvious in 21:8 and 21:23. But it is also a promise that accompanies the call to be holy. It is a promise that, as already noted in the previous chapter, as God's people strive to be holy they are not alone, that God is also working in and among them to make them holy.

Church Leaders

As with the priests, church leaders are especially responsible for the way they behave. They are shepherds and, like the keepers of sheep of Bible times, they are to lead by example rather than drive by force. They will be answerable to the Chief Shepherd when he returns (1 Peter 5:2-4). They have been given leadership gifts and a great deal will be expected of them in the way those gifts are used (Luke 12:48). Those who have been given the gift of teaching will be judged more strictly than those they teach (James 3:1). The example that church leaders set must match the teaching they give. Paul told Timothy to "set the believers an example in speech, in conduct, in love, in faith, in purity" (1 Timothy 4:12). So the church leader must live a life that is above reproach (1 Timothy 3:2-3).

A Church Leader and his Family

Perhaps the most notorious way in which a church leader can lose credibility is in the manner in which he conducts his family. Paul stipulates that church leaders should have only one wife (1 Timothy 3:2, 12; Titus 1:6). It may not be so necessary to say that in these days, bigamy being illegal, but in Bible times families with more than one wife were not peaceful but generally noted for rivalry and jealousy both between the wives and between the children. What is a necessary command these days is that a church leader should be careful to marry a woman who is a Christian and in full support of her husband in the work he has to do (2 Corinthians 6:14).

Another requirement that is essential to reiterate is that he should keep his children in order. Priests had to do so (Leviticus 21:9). If a church leader cannot do that, how can he care properly for God's church? (1 Timothy 3:4-5, 12)

No Favouritism

It may have been a temptation in Moses' time for a priest to give relatives and friends special treatment. It may have seemed easier to allow someone to eat the priests' food who was not entitled to do so than to withstand the pleas of, say, a married daughter. A priest may have had to deal with a relative or a particular friend trying to persuade him to accept for sacrifice an animal that was not perfect.

Church leaders must show no favouritism. For this reason, in many church constitutions it stipulates that two or more members who are of the same family or who are related by marriage may not serve as church officers at the same time. Family loyalty has often proved stronger than the desire to do what is right. Jesus said that devotion to him must come first (Matthew 10:37).

Jude writes to warn about some who have entered the church fellowship who seek to lead by "showing favouritism to gain advantage" (Jude 1:16). There is a need to be wary of those who do not treat everyone equally.

Believers as Priests

God barred from approaching him descendants of Aaron who had physical blemishes. But when he came to earth in the person of Jesus of Nazareth everything changed. In response to a comment concerning the privilege of sitting at table in the kingdom of God, Jesus told a parable about people being invited to a great banquet, but, when the time came, those who had been invited made excuses for not attending. So servants were sent out to the slums to bring in the poor, the crippled, the blind and the lame (Luke 14:15-24). Such people, it seems, would be welcome in God's kingdom. During the week before the crucifixion the blind and the lame came to Jesus in the temple and there he healed them (Matthew 21:14).

The physical is symbolic of the spiritual. Those who would enter God's presence must have "clean hands and a pure heart" (Psalm 24:3-4). Our spiritual imperfections form a barrier between us and God. But those who put their faith and trust in the Lord Jesus Christ are given right of access into God's presence (Romans 5:1-2). The Church is "a holy priesthood" (1 Peter 2:5). Every believer may with confidence "enter the holy places by the blood of Jesus" (Hebrews 10:19).

Responsibilities of Believers

It follows that many of those things required of the priests relate, not only to church leaders, but to all believers.

As the priests had to avoid appearing to approve of pagan practices, so Christians must be careful to avoid becoming closely associated with those who consistently disobey God (Ephesians 5:6-7). Their task is to expose evil practices without becoming involved in them (Ephesians 5:11).

The priests had to limit their involvement in funerals so that their ability to serve God would not be restricted. The service of God had to come first. Christ's requirement that devotion to him must take precedence over family ties applies to all Christians not just to leaders (Matthew 10:37).

127

The question of quality or quantity is one that should concern Christians. Often the impression is given that the more church services attended, or the more Bible study is undertaken, or the more time is spent in prayer, the better pleased God will be. Jesus said that pagans thought that the longer their prayers the more likely their gods would listen to them, and he told his disciples not to be like them. Jesus went on to teach them a pattern for prayer which is very brief but covers everything necessary (Matthew 6:7-13). Quality is more important than quantity.

God told Israel that he was the one who was making them holy. Christians are called to strive for holiness (Hebrews 12:14) and to work their salvation out in their daily lives (Philippians 2:12). But we do not have to do so on our own and solely by our own efforts. God is at work in us to make us willing and able to obey Him (Philippians 2:13) and to make us like His Son (Romans 8:28-29).

Our Great High Priest

The chief priest of Leviticus points to our great high priest, Jesus, the Son of God (Hebrews 4:14). He was faithful in every way (Hebrews 3:1-2) never leaving the sanctuary, remaining in unbroken, obedient fellowship with His Father until the work was done. He was obedient to death on a cross in order to present the sacrifice of Himself on our behalf (Hebrews 9:26).

He has chosen a bride for Himself, the Church (Revelation 19:7-9). One day He will take her to Himself and, like a virgin, she will be "without spot or wrinkle or any such thing", "holy and without blemish" (Ephesians 5:27). The confident hope of every individual believer is that all imperfections will be removed. When Jesus comes again He will change even weak, imperfect bodies to be like his glorious, resurrection body. The body represents the whole person. We will be completely and perfectly fitted to spend eternity in His presence, in the Most Holy Place. So we eagerly await the return of our Saviour (Philippians 3:20-21).

Celebrations
Leviticus 23

It is obvious that marking the occurrence of events with dates is essential in today's world. The reasons are practical. But the reasons for annual celebrations of certain events are more to do with hearts and minds.

Until 1834, bank holidays were observed by the Bank of England and numbered thirty-three. These included saints' days, Good Friday and Christmas Day. So the reasons for keeping these days as holidays were religious. Since then various Acts of Parliament have reduced then increased the number, so that, in 2016, it stands at eight. The religious reasons for observing Good Friday and Christmas Day have, for most people, disappeared, but the holidays are still observed. Christmas Day may be an excuse to brighten up the home at the time of year when daylight hours are short, but most people are thinking about presents, food and drink, and TV.

For Christians, the Christmas holidays are an opportunity to remember the wonder of the Incarnation, and the Easter weekend is an opportunity to meditate on the death and resurrection of the Saviour. These festivals may serve a useful purpose for Christians, but they are creations of man. They were given a Christian flavour, in the first place by the Bank of England, no doubt with the approval and encouragement of the established church. The difference between these festivals and those of Israel is that the latter were given by God; they were "the appointed feasts of the LORD" (2, 4, 37, 44).

Holy Gatherings

The times of celebration that God appointed were to be "holy convocations" (2). While in the wilderness it would be relatively practical for everybody to gather together, presumably around the Tabernacle. After they had settled in the Promised Land, spread out and grown in number, most of the gatherings would be local, eventually at the synagogues, but for three of the feasts it was required that all men must go to the central place of worship (Deuteronomy 16:16).

The gatherings were to be holy. The purpose was not simply an opportunity for them to meet up with friends and family, but that they should meet with God. There were sacrifices to be offered, more details of which are given in Numbers 28-29 for the benefit of officiating priests. As time went by the gatherings included reading and explaining the Scriptures (Deuteronomy

31:10-13). So the purpose of these holy convocations was that the whole nation should be united in the worship of God.

Sabbath (3)

The seventh day had been established from Creation as a day of rest (Genesis 2:2-3). After their escape from Egypt, the Israelites learned by experience that they could rest on the seventh day in the confidence that God would supply their needs during the six preceding days (Exodus 16). This was in total contrast to the 24/7 round of slavery in Egypt.

From the Ten Commandments they learned that not only should they rest from work but they must ensure that their servants, their employees, also had a day off work (Exodus 20:9-11). They were not to treat others as they had been treated when they were slaves.

Then in Leviticus 23 they were told the positive aspect of the Sabbath. It was to be a day of "holy convocation", a coming together to worship their Creator and remember that he had rescued them from the non-stop grind of slavery.

Passover and Unleavened Bread (4-8)

The first Passover was the meal eaten in the evening of the last day the Hebrews spent in Egypt. The meal was eaten in family homes. The centre-piece of the meal was the lamb, the blood of which had been collected in a basin and daubed on the doorframe of the house. God had promised, "When I see the blood, I will pass over you" (Exodus 12:13). Those who were in the houses where the blood was displayed were protected when God passed through Egypt killing all the firstborn. Another part of the meal was unleavened bread (Exodus 12:8). It was unleavened because they were about to leave Egypt in a hurry and there would be no time to allow the dough to rise. Until they had really escaped and were able to settle into a routine, they would continue to eat bread that was unleavened. These two aspects of their rescue from slavery were to be celebrated annually (Exodus 12:14-20).

This annual celebration is reaffirmed in Leviticus 23. The Passover meal was to be eaten in the evening of the fourteenth day of the first month (5). This was to be followed by the Feast of Unleavened Bread which was to last for seven days. On the first day all leaven was to be removed from their homes and they were to ensure that no leaven was to be found there for the entire week (Exodus 12:15, 19). At the Passover and during the following seven days only unleavened bread was to be eaten.

It is evident that, by New Testament times, in Jewish thought they formed one festival. It was on "the first day of Unleavened Bread" that the disciples asked Jesus where He wanted them to prepare to eat the Passover (Matthew 26:17). Luke refers to "the Feast of Unleavened Bread ... which is called the Passover" (Luke 22:7). This two-in-one festival was to be a reminder of two features of the Exodus, the blood of the lamb and the unleavened bread.

This was the first of the three feasts for which all men had to go to the central place of worship (Deuteronomy 16:16).

The purpose of these celebrations was not to remember Moses' great leadership or their own shaking off of the shackles of Egypt, or even the destruction of the Egypt army as they attempted to cross the Red Sea. This was to be "the LORD's Passover" (5). It was a reminder that God had struck Egypt with the plagues and had provided the means of salvation for His people. The first and last days of Unleavened Bread were to be holy convocations and every day sacrifices were to be offered to God (Numbers 28:19-25). The focus was on God and what He had done.

The Day of Firstfruits (9-14)

This was a celebration that looked forward to the time when they were settled in Canaan (10). That was also true of Pentecost (15-22), and Booths (33-43).

It was essentially an acknowledgement of God's provision in the grain harvests, in particular the barley harvest. The day is fixed by the phrase "the day after the Sabbath" (11), where the Sabbath referred to is the first day of Unleavened Bread. So Passover, Unleavened Bread and Firstfruits were all celebrated within one week.

This was an individual event for each farmer to bring to the priest at the tabernacle a sheaf of the first of his crop to ripen (10). The priest had to wave the sheaf in God's presence (11) as a symbol that it was being given to God. This had to be done if the worshipper was to be "accepted" (11). This probably refers to the fact that, until the sheaf of firstfruits was offered, they were not allowed to eat of the new harvest themselves (14). On the same day as the sheaf of grain was offered, a year-old lamb had to be given as a burnt offering (12), along with a grain offering and a drink offering (13).

The pagans went to extreme lengths to try to persuade their gods to give them a good harvest. God promised His people that if they lived in obedience to Him, He would always provide plenty (Deuteronomy 28:1-14). So they were to trust Him to provide and then present their firstfruits to Him in acknowledgement of His provision and as an expression of thanks.

The Day of Pentecost (15-22)

This feast is not given a name here, but is called the Feast of Weeks in Deuteronomy 16:10. It is so called because the day was fixed by counting seven weeks from the day of Firstfruits (15). In the New Testament it is called Pentecost from the Greek word meaning fiftieth, the fiftieth day counting from and including the day of Firstfruits.

Pentecost celebrated the completed grain harvest of barley and wheat. This was the second of the three feasts for which all men had to attend the central place of worship (Deuteronomy 16:16). Each household had to provide two loaves of bread to be given as a gift to God (17). These would be food for the priests.

The animals required for sacrifice on that day comprised seven year-old lambs, one bull and two rams for a burnt offering (18), accompanied by grain and drink offerings. In addition God required one male goat for a sin offering and two year-old male lambs for a peace offering (19).

No instructions are given as to who was to provide these offerings. But in Deuteronomy 16:16-17 the instructions are given that the men "shall not appear before the LORD empty-handed", but that each one should give as he was able, according to how much God had blessed him. One would expect that if those instructions were observed there would be enough to provide the sacrifices required.

As with Firstfruits, this was an acknowledgement of God's provision and an expression of thanks.

Verse 22 is an abbreviated version of the rules in 19:9-10. It is a reminder that if their relationship with God is real it will show in their attitude towards others; giving to God must be matched by generosity towards those less fortunate than themselves.

Trumpets (23-25)

Two silver trumpets were made. When both were blown together it was a call for all the people to gather at the tent of meeting (Numbers 10:1-3). On the first day of the seventh month the trumpets were to be blown to call the people to a day of rest and a holy convocation (24).

The trumpet blast also served as "a memorial" (24). When God descended on Mount Sinai to give Moses the Law, the occasion was marked by "a very loud trumpet blast" (Exodus 19:16). So the trumpets would remind the people of the covenant made at Sinai. On the other hand, God told Moses that blowing the trumpets on special occasions would be "a reminder of you before your God" (Numbers 10:10). God said that when they went into battle they were to sound the trumpets "that you may be remembered before the LORD your God, and you shall be saved from your enemies" (Numbers 10:9). So the blast of the two trumpets was like a two-way prayer, the people and their God remembering the two sides of the covenant between them.

On this day they were to present a food offering to the LORD (25). The details of the burnt offering, grain offerings and sin offering required are given in Numbers 19:1-6 for the benefit of the officiating priests.

The Day of Atonement (26-32)

The Day of Atonement was to be observed on the tenth day of the seventh month. Detailed instructions for the high priest were given in Leviticus 16. Those instructions included what was required by way of "a food offering" (27).

The instructions in chapter 23 are for the people. Three times they are told they must afflict themselves (27, 29, 32). Three times they are told that they must do no work (28, 30, 31). And they are warned of the consequences of disobeying (29, 30). This day must be taken seriously because if atonement was not made for them before the LORD their God (28), then the special relationship between them and God would cease and God's provision and protection would come to an end. Five days later the third feast at which all men must appear at the central sanctuary would take place, so it was essential that sanctuary and people were fit for that week of celebrating in God's presence.

The Feast of Booths (33-43)

This was the third feast listed in Deuteronomy 16:16, and the last in the year. It began on the fifteenth day of the tenth month. The first day was a day of rest and holy gathering together (35), and the feast was drawn to a close in the same way on the eighth day (36).

133

Sacrifices were to be offered every day (36). The animals required for each day are set out in Numbers 29:12-38. Over the course of the eight days a total of seventy-one bulls, fifteen rams, ninety-one year-old male lambs and eight goats were required. These were to be accompanied by grain offerings amounting to at least one hundred kilos of fine flour. This huge demand, when compared with the sacrifices required on other occasions, indicates that Booths was probably the most important feast of the year.

For seven days everybody had to live in temporary shelters to remind them of the time that had been spent in the wilderness on the way from Egypt to the Promised Land (42, 43). The shelters were to be made using branches of trees and palms (40). When the feast began the dates, the figs and the pomegranates would have been harvested and the grape harvest would be well under way. It seems that the shelters were to be decorated with some of the harvested fruit (40). It was a time of great rejoicing (40) as they remembered how God had provided for them in the wilderness and had continued to provide up to that present year.

Sevens

The number seven occurs frequently in these celebrations. There are seven festivals, Passover, Unleavened Bread, Firstfruits, Pentecost, Trumpets, Atonement and Booths. Apart from the weekly Sabbath there were seven special days of rest, the first day and last day of Unleavened Bread (7, 8), the Day of Pentecost (21), the first day of the seventh month (24-25), the Day of Atonement (28), the first day of the Feast of Booths (35), and the day after that feast had finished (36).

The seventh month is selected for special mention in that, although the trumpets were to be blown on many occasions through the course of the year, it is only their use on the first day of the seventh month that is mentioned here. During the seventh month the two festivals were held which were arguably the most important of all, the Day of Atonement and the Feast of Booths.

So week after week, festival after festival, year after year, these sevens reminded the Israelites of their Creator God, of all that He had done and had promised to do for them, and their duty to meet the needs of others, in particular in allowing them frequent and regular days of rest.

A New Number

In Leviticus the eighth day often signals a new beginning. It was the day Aaron began his duties as High Priest (9:1). It was the day when a male baby was to be circumcised (12:30) and became a new member of the nation of Israel. People cleansed of leprosy (14:10 and 23) or of discharges (15:14 and 29) were presented before the LORD on the eighth day so that they could renew lives of fellowship with him. Following the Feast of Booths, the eighth day signalled that one agricultural year had ended and a new one had begun.

New beginnings on the eighth day are recorded in the New Testament. Jesus rose from the dead on the first day of the week, the eighth day. The Church began at Pentecost, another eighth day. Because of these events, the Church began the tradition of meeting on the first day of the week.

One day of rest in every seven meets a need that is human not merely religious. That is evident from the fact that it was established at Creation not only given in the Ten Commandments. It interrupts the constant drive to make money and the exploitation of others, it provides an opportunity to think of things that last, it is a reminder of the Creator God who is the very source of life itself, and it gives opportunity and incentive to renew one's relationship with Him.

Annual celebrations such as Christmas, Lent, Easter, Whitsun and Harvest can be helpful if they turn our thoughts and behaviour Godward. But if observing them is made a legal requirement, the observation becomes an end in itself, and the meaning, purpose and benefit are lost. The same applies to the observance of Sunday. Paul's appeal not to judge another who does not have the same attitude as we do to days we consider special, must be borne in mind (Romans 14:4-7).

Shadows and Reality

Jesus died at Passover. He is our "Passover lamb" who "has been sacrificed for us" (1 Corinthians 5:7). He rose again on the day after the Sabbath, on the day on which the sheaves of the firstfruits of the barley harvest were presented to God. He is "the firstfruits of those who have fallen asleep" (1 Corinthians 15:20).

Seven weeks later, on the day of Pentecost, when the Jews were celebrating God's gift of the complete grain harvest, the promised gift of the

Holy Spirit was given and there was a great harvest of souls – three thousand were added to the Church (Acts 2:1-4, 41).

As on the Day of Atonement the high priest entered the Most Holy Place, so Christ has entered, thus making a way into God's presence for us (Hebrews 10:19-20). One day the trumpet that reminds of the covenant and rallies God's people will sound. Those who are Christ's through the New Covenant, both those who are alive and those who have fallen asleep, will be called together to meet the Lord. We will be with him forever (1 Thessalonians 4:16-17).

The Feast of Booths was a time of great rejoicing in the LORD because, through His goodness all harvests were safely gathered in and the year's work was done. The marriage supper of the Lamb will be a time of great rejoicing; it will signal the completion of God's work of salvation in the Bride, the Church (Revelation 19:7-9).

Meanwhile

We live in a time, as it were, of "unleavened bread". As the Israelites were to ensure at the start of the Feast of Unleavened Bread that no leaven was left in their homes, so we are to "cleanse out the old leaven … of malice and evil" and ensure that our lives are filled with "the unleavened bread of sincerity and truth" (1 Corinthians 5:7-8).

The Israelites were to ensure that in their rejoicing over God's provision they did not forget the poor. They were to leave some of the harvest for the poor to glean (23:22). We also must remember that everything we have is from God, given to enable us to meet the needs of those less fortunate than ourselves (James 1:17, 27).

A Special Relationship
Leviticus 24

Between the United Kingdom and the United States of America there is a special relationship. The expression is commonly associated with a speech made by Winston Churchill in 1946, but the relationship has been in evidence since the nineteenth century. It has been displayed in various ways, especially in fighting together in several wars in the twentieth century, and now, in the twenty-first century, fighting against terrorism. It is a relationship that is called upon from time to time for mutual benefit. It has not always been marked by friendship. There have been incidents which have led some in the UK to conclude that the USA is unreliable, and some in the USA to say the same of the British.

In contrast to that, the special relationship between God and Israel was one of God's choosing and making. It was a relationship which brought great benefits to Israel but, on God's part, He entered into it simply because He loved them (Deuteronomy 7:7-8). It was Israel that proved to be unreliable while God has remained eternally faithful to His covenant.

The system of feasts detailed in Leviticus 23 gave opportunities to express that relationship regularly, every week and every year. But the instructions of chapter 24 show that the special relationship between God and Israel was in effect all the time, and had to be respected all day every day. That is shown in the rules about two symbols, the lamps and the loaves, and in the historical record of a man cursing God.

The Lamps (2-4)

Light was the first thing God created (Genesis 1:3), and it is essential to life. When Pharaoh opposed God and refused to set the Hebrews free, God withdrew light from Egypt (Exodus 10:22-23) as a precursor to the death of the firstborn. On the other hand, God is good to His people by "lifting up the light of [his] face" upon them (Psalm 4:6). Where the Hebrew slaves were living there was light (Exodus 10:23), and in the wilderness He gave them light at night by a pillar of fire (Exodus 13:21). To serve as a perpetual reminder of these things, a gold lampstand was made to give light in the tabernacle.

Directions for making the lampstand (4) are recorded in Exodus 25:31-39. It was made of pure gold and had seven branches, each made to support a lamp. Each lamp was a gold bowl with its rim partially pinched together to leave a small hole to support the wick and a larger hole to allow for replenishing with oil. The lampstand stood in the outer section of the tabernacle, the Holy Place, and on the south side, that is, on the left as the priest faced the veil before the Most Holy Place.

The lamps were to be attended to every evening so that they would give light all through the night (3; cf. 1 Samuel 3:3). Man's work comes to an end at sunset (Psalm 104:23) but the light of God shines on. So David was able to say that he could sleep in peace because the LORD would keep him safe (Psalm 4:8). Pilgrims on the road to Jerusalem would sing, "He who keeps Israel will neither slumber nor sleep" (Psalm 121:4).

The people were involved in this symbolic expression of their relationship with God. They had to beat the olives, they had to ensure that the oil was pure, and they had to bring the oil to Moses (2). Aaron had to tend the lamps every day (3-4). In doing all this the whole nation was acknowledging its dependence upon God for light and life and every good thing.

The Loaves (5-9)

Bread was seen as a gift of God in a very special way. It required a successful grain harvest which depended on the rains coming at the right time. These things were seen to be in the hands of God and one's "daily bread" recognised as a regular reminder of His gracious care.

In the Bible the Hebrew and Greek words for "bread" are often used to refer to food in general, for example in Genesis 28:20 and in 2 Thessalonians 3:8. In the Middle East the giving and accepting of "bread", whether a complete meal or merely a piece of bread, has been seen as a symbol of hospitality and friendship. To accept that hospitality and so enter into friendship but then to be disloyal was the highest insult and offence. That is why David was so shocked that his friend, one who had eaten his bread, had turned against him (Psalm 41:9).

It was against this sort of background that God commanded that twelve loaves of bread should be on display in the tabernacle (5). The God-given instructions for the construction of a table of wood overlaid with gold are recorded in Exodus 25:23-30. The table was God's table. It was to stand in the Holy Place opposite the golden lampstand, and the twelve loaves were to be arranged on the table in two rows (or piles) of six with some frankincense for each row (6-7). Every Sabbath (8) the frankincense would be burnt on the altar as "a memorial portion" (7), new loaves and fresh frankincense would be arranged on the table, and the old loaves would be eaten by Aaron and his sons (9).

The bread was "the bread of the Presence" so God was there. God was inviting His people to a perpetual, symbolic meal of friendship and, by supplying the loaves (8), the people were accepting that invitation. The whole nation was there because each tribe was represented by one of the twelve loaves. All day every day God and His people were, in symbol, sharing bread at God's table and confirming the special relationship between them.

The Name (10-23)

The special relationship between God and the nation had personal connotations, as the story of the fighting and cursing shows. Any individual who offended against God's laws would also be breaking the laws of the community and would be setting himself apart from both God and the people. For them the special relationship would be destroyed.

What the cause was of the fight between the man of mixed race and the Israelite (10) we are not told. Perhaps the Israelite taunted the other for his mixed parentage and he reacted in the only way he knew. He is not rebuked for fighting but for the fact that he "blasphemed the Name and cursed" (11).

The Name, Yahweh, was not merely a label. It means "I am who I am" (Exodus 3:14), which means that God will be known by what he does (Exodus 3:16). That means that it stands for what God is like (Exodus 34:6-7) and so stands for God himself (Jeremiah 23:27). In blaspheming and cursing God's Name, the man was attacking God Himself as if by doing so he would deprive the Israelite of his source of strength.

Those who heard him curse brought him to Moses. It seems that this had not happened before because, although they knew from the third commandment that misusing God's name was a punishable offence, even Moses did not know exactly what to do. So, very sensibly, they waited for God to make known His will (12). We are not told how long they had to wait or what means God used, but when the answer came it was unequivocal. The offender must be put to death.

God told Moses this (14), and instructed him to tell the people (15), so that the whole nation would know. Everybody was to be involved in the rejection of this sin. The man was to be taken out of the camp. Those who had heard him curse were to lay their hands on his head as if even the memory of those words needed to be rejected and cleansed away (14). "All the congregation" was to be involved in the stoning (14 and 16). Condoning the man's behaviour would have resulted in the relationship between God and the nation being broken.

By repeating the law that whoever takes human life must be put to death (17), God makes it clear that to "blaspheme the Name" is as serious as murder. He goes on to remind them that in every case, including blasphemy, the punishment must fit the crime (18-21). This rule must be applied whether the offender is an Israelite, a half-caste or a foreigner (16 and 22). Human affections and relationships must not stand in the way of doing God's will. The special relationship between Israel and God must be preserved.

The Light of the World

The light of the lampstand was no more than a symbol of the presence of God. But the message of John the Baptist was that the true light was coming into the world (John 1:6-9). Jesus said that he had come into the world as light (John 12:46). He was the true light in that He was not merely a symbol of God's presence, He was Immanuel, God actually with us (Matthew 1:23).

He came, not simply to stay in one building for priests of one nation to see, but as the light of the world (John 8:12) and promised that any who followed Him would have the light of life. Just as the light of the sun makes life possible, so the Lord Jesus gives life. That life is eternal life, God's life that, for those who believe in Jesus, begins in the here and now and will never end (John 11:25-26).

We have all, in small ways or big, insulted God by disobeying his laws. We deserve the darkness of death meted out to the one who cursed the LORD. Jesus has borne the darkness for us, as was illustrated by the three hours of darkness that He endured on the Cross (Luke 23:44-45).

Paul described himself as the worst of sinners because, he said, he had been a blasphemer, a persecutor, an opponent of Christ (1 Timothy 1:13-15). But, on the road to Damascus, Jesus confronted him in a dazzling light from heaven (Acts 9:1-6). He was physically blind for a short while but later he was able to write that the God who created light had shone in his heart "to give the light of the knowledge of the glory of God in the face of Jesus Christ" (2 Corinthians 4:6).

As we come to Christ and accept the light of life that He is, we enter into a special relationship with God and are able to say that "our fellowship is with the Father and with his Son Jesus Christ" (1 John 1:3). If we would have that relationship remain unbroken we must "walk in the light" (1 John 1:7). In particular, we must love one another, that is, we must be willing to lay down our lives to meet the needs of one another (John 15:12-13; 1 John 2:9-10). In this way we will be following our Lord, being lights of the world ourselves (Matthew 5:14).

An Open Invitation

The bread of the Presence was to be eaten by Aaron and his sons in a holy place (9). But when David was on the run from Saul, Abimelech the priest gave the bread to him and his men (1 Samuel 21:1-6). Jesus used that fact to answer the Pharisees when they criticised him for allowing his disciples to "harvest" corn on the Sabbath (Matthew 12:1-4). God "desires mercy and not sacrifice" (Matthew 12:7). He is more concerned about meeting the needs of his people than preserving religious ritual. That being so, who is welcome at God's table?

The religious leaders in the time of Jesus were quite sure that sinners, such as tax-collectors, were excluded from the Kingdom of God. But when Jesus called Levi to leave his tax-collecting and follow him, Levi made a great feast and invited many other tax-collectors and disreputable people (Luke 5:27-32). Jesus ate with those men. On another occasion Jesus called Zacchaeus, a tax-collector, down from a tree and spent the day at Zacchaeus' house (Luke 19:1-10). Sinners who respond to Jesus' call are forgiven and made fit to have table fellowship with him.

The religious leaders were equally certain that those with diseases and deformities were also excluded. However, in the parable about the banquet and those who made excuses (Luke 14:16-24) it was those of whom the Jews would have thought acceptable, the well-to-do and respectable, that were invited initially. But in the end it was "the poor and crippled and blind and lame" who occupied the places and enjoyed the feast.

In Matthew's account of this parable (Matthew 22:1-14) Jesus tells of a man who came to the banquet without bothering to change into clean clothes. This was a huge insult and the man was thrown out. The invitation is open to any who will accept it, but those who would eat at the table must be clean.

141

Jesus enjoyed a meal at the home of Simon whom He had, it seems, healed of leprosy (Matthew 14:3). He heals and cleanses those who come to Him. Any who accept His invitation He makes fit to sit at God's table.

The Jews thought that the blessing of sitting at table in God's kingdom was exclusively for them. But Jesus said that people would come from all over the world to eat at God's table. To emphasise how welcome they would be, Jesus said that even despised Gentiles would be feasting alongside the revered forefathers of the Jews, Abraham, Isaac and Jacob (Matthew 8:11).

The Name High Over All

Joseph was told that the child that Mary would bear must be called Jesus. This was because of what He would do; He would save His people from their sins (Matthew 1:21). It was also because of who He was; Jesus means "Yahweh (the LORD) is salvation". Those who call upon His name are calling upon the person that name represents, that person who is the only means of salvation (Acts 4:12).

Those who, in response to the apostles' teaching, desired to obey the Lord Jesus were to be baptised into the name of the Father, the Son and the Holy Spirit (Matthew 28:18). They would bear His name and therefore become His property (2 Timothy 2:19) and so enter into a special relationship with God. They would become known as those who "call upon the name of our Lord Jesus Christ" (1 Corinthians 1:2). When they meet in His name, even when they are few in number, He is there to guide and answer prayer (Matthew 18:19-20).

That name represents great power and authority. Because Jesus was totally obedient, even to death on a cross, God gave Him "the name that is above every name, so that at the name of Jesus every knee should bow" (Philippians 2:6-11). This is in fulfilment of the prophecy of Isaiah 45:23 where the LORD says that every knee will bow to Him. It means that Jesus has been given the greatest possible authority (Matthew 28:18), and everything and everybody will have to submit to His will.

So Jesus was able to promise His disciples that if when they prayed they were to do so in the name of Jesus, they could be sure of an answer (John 14:13-14) because the prayer would carry all the authority of the Lord Jesus Himself. In the same way, by invoking the name of Jesus they could perform miracles (Acts 3:6-7), because by using His name they were calling upon his power.

The name of Jesus cannot be used as a magic spell. When some Jews tried to use the name of Jesus to perform an exorcism, they found that instead of having power over the evil spirit it was able to overpower them (Acts 19:13). To them "Jesus" was just a word. They had no special relationship with the real person of Jesus, so were not actually calling upon Him, and they were unable to claim His authority. They misused the Name and suffered the consequences.

Walk Worthy

The annual church calendar can be helpful as a reminder of the truths of the Gospel, of what God has done and is doing through His Son Jesus and by His Spirit. Sunday services are opportunities to encourage one another (Hebrews 10:25) and to prepare for the week ahead. But our special relationship with the Lord does not consist in such religious observances. It is a relationship that exists and demands our respect twenty-four hours a day, seven days a week. We are to live in a manner that is "worthy of the Lord". That means that what we do and say, and even what we think should be "fully pleasing to Him" (Colossians 1:10; Philippians 4:8).

Living in a way that is worthy of and faithful to the Name we bear is never easy. The Lord Jesus commended the Christians in Pergamum because, He said, "You hold fast to my name." This was in spite of great pressure to deny Him; Jesus said that Pergamum was "where Satan dwells", and at least one of them had been killed for being faithful to his Lord (Revelation 2:13).

Many in the world today are facing the choice of either denying their Saviour and saving their lives, or being faithful to the Name and losing their lives. The apostles rejoiced because they had been considered worthy to suffer for the Name (Acts 5:41).

Jesus said, "Whoever would save his life will lose it, but whoever loses his life for my sake and the gospel's will save it." (Mark 8:35).

Rest and Restoration
Leviticus 25

Many third world countries spend almost half their budget repaying foreign debt, with the result that they are unable to provide even basic health care for their children. The interest demanded on the debts is such that some countries have already paid back more than they borrowed yet still owe many times the initial loan. If their debts are not forgiven, they will sink into complete destitution.

The late Dr Martin Dent realised this and, in 1990 he, together with a group of his students at Keele University, signed a petition calling for those debts to be cancelled. In 1993 the late William Peters, a retired diplomat, joined forces with Dr Dent and together they founded the Jubilee 2000 Drop the Debt Campaign. The concept was founded on Leviticus 25 and the aim was to have third world debt written off by the Millenium.

The experience of nations in debt is mirrored by the experience of individuals who borrow to solve a financial problem but then find that paying off the loan becomes a problem from which there is no escape. God's people were to cancel all debts every seventh year (Deuteronomy 15:1-11). The aim of the instructions in Leviticus 25 was to provide a way out for individual Israelites who, through poverty, had sold their land and may even have gone so far as to sell themselves into slavery.

The Agricultural Year

The religious year for the Israelites began with the month in which the Passover was to be celebrated (Exodus 12:2). That month came to be known as Nisan and equates to the second half of March and the first half of April.

On the other hand, their agricultural year began sometime after the Feast of Booths at which the completed harvest of that year's produce was celebrated. During the last few months of the religious year, when the showers of October/November had softened the ground, the land would be prepared, and seed for barley and wheat would be sown. Since the sowing of seed is forbidden in both the Sabbatical year (4) and the Jubilee year (11), it is obvious that it is the agricultural year which is meant in this chapter.

Rest for the land

The chapter begins with a reminder of the rule recorded in Exodus 23:10-11, that every seventh year would be a Sabbatical year and the land must be allowed to lie fallow. During the Sabbatical year the people were not to harvest their fields or clear their vines with a view to storing the produce for the weeks and months ahead. Instead, from whatever the land produced without cultivation, they were to gather and pick enough to meet their immediate, daily needs. Animals were to be free to feed themselves and the poor were to have as easy access to the food as the rich (Exodus 23:11). So, for that year, the differences between the haves and have-nots would be imperceptible.

The land lying fallow for a year would tend to replenish itself naturally and help to avoid its becoming a dust bowl as the prairies of North America did in the 1930s. The Sabbatical year would provide a time of rest for the people from the constant struggle to survive. It would remind them that the land belonged to God (23). It would demand from them confidence that, because they were His people, God would provide for them (21). So there would be spiritual benefits as well as physical.

The Jubilee Year

In the seventh Sabbatical year (8), the trumpet was to be blown on the Day of Atonement (9) to announce the coming Jubilee year (11). In that year, the fiftieth (10), as in the Sabbatical year, the land was to lie fallow (11-12). This would mean that the Israelites would have to live on whatever was left from what they had harvested in the sixth year, and on what they could gather growing wild, for two consecutive years.

This seems an excessively long time and has led some to say that the Jubilee year was the seventh Sabbatical year, the forty-ninth year. But, although the question of verse 20 is about what they will eat in the seventh year, God promises a crop in the sixth year that will be sufficient for three years (21), enough to see them through until the harvest of the ninth year (22). The variation in the timing of the rains and the amount of rainfall does, in fact, lead to big differences in the sizes of harvests. So, with God's over-ruling, surviving for three years on the harvest of one year plus what they could gather, would not have been a problem. The message of verses 18-19 is completely clear. If they obeyed God's commands they would eat their fill and be secure.

The trumpet was to be blown on the Day of Atonement when their sins of the past year had been dealt with. They knew that their relationship with God was right and nothing was standing in the way of His blessing (Deuteronomy

28:1-6). Five days later they would celebrate the Feast of Booths when they would be reminded of God's gracious provision. So they were given every reason to be confident that God would provide for their needs during the coming years.

The Meaning of "Jubilee"

The meaning of the Hebrew word translated "jubilee" is uncertain. The blowing of the trumpet was to be followed by a proclamation of liberty (10) and the Greek version of Leviticus 25 uses a word for "jubilee" which means "release". The Jubilee was to be a year of release from debt and from slavery, a year of freedom to return to one's property and clan (10).

It was inevitable that, from time to time, Israelites would "become poor" (25, 35, 39, 47). Whatever the cause of an Israelite's financial problems, and whatever means he had taken to solve those problems, whether by selling his property (25-31), or by selling his labour as a hired worker (35-38), or by selling himself as a slave (39-55), at Jubilee the slate was wiped clean, everybody was given a new start. It would bring to an end any process of the rich getting richer and the poor getting poorer.

Selling Their Property (25-31)

Property was seen to be held in trust from God because the land belonged to Him (23), and was to be divided up between the tribes at God's direction (Joshua 13 to 19). Because of this, no Israelite would sell his property except as a last resort when he had fallen on hard times. Land must never be sold in perpetuity (23). God's purpose was that sooner or later the property would be returned to the original owner either by redemption (24) or in the year of Jubilee (28).

When property was sold, buyer and seller had to arrange a price based on the number of years after the Jubilee (15). The price was to be calculated according to the number of harvests that the buyer could expect to get from the land (15-16) before the next Jubilee, when the land would cease to be his (28). In this way they would avoid wronging one another (14, 17). There would be no speculative buying, no profiteering.

The possibility of redeeming the property must always be open (24). The closest relative of the original owner had this responsibility (25). If the circumstances of the original owner improved so that he could afford to buy back his property, he had to pay a proportion of the price he was paid according to the number of years since he sold it (26-27). Thus if he had sold the land five years previously and fifteen years remained until Jubilee, he would have to pay back seventy-five percent of the purchase price. The temporary owner would not profit from escalating house prices.

If neither the original owner nor a close relative were able to redeem the property, he had to wait until Jubilee (28) when it would be returned without payment.

Exceptions (29-34)

The above rules related to fields and houses in villages or in the open country (31). If a house within a walled city was sold, redemption was allowed within one year of the sale. Once a year had passed, redemption was no longer permitted and it was not returned to the original owner at Jubilee. It became the purchaser's property in perpetuity (29-30). Houses in walled towns were not closely attached to the land which provided the all-important food for man and beast.

The houses of Levites were in forty-eight walled towns and the surrounding land was theirs to use for pasture (Numbers 35:1-8). If they sold their houses they could be redeemed at any time, or they would be returned to them in Jubilee (32-33). But the pasture-lands surrounding the towns must never be sold; God had given them to the Levites as a permanent possession (34). The Levites were not given any other land of their own (Joshua 14:4), so these rules ensured that they were not left with nowhere to pasture their animals.

Selling Their Labour (35-38)

If an Israelite's financial problems were not solved by selling his property, he could sell his labour to a fellow Israelite in exchange for bed and board. He was to be treated with the same hospitality as would have been shown to any visitor (35). The host was not to make any profit from his stay. If he lent him money, he was not to charge interest and he was not to charge for his food (37). The host was to treat his visitor as if they were two brothers living together (36).

Selling Themselves to a Relative (39-46)

If selling his labour did not solve the Israelite's financial problems, he could sell himself to a relative. This would provide a lump sum rather than income and he might be able to clear his debts immediately. He was to be treated as a hired worker. This meant that he could not be forced to do work that was excessively strenuous (43, 46). His period of service was limited to six years and in the seventh he was to be given the opportunity to go free (Deuteronomy 15:12-18). In Jubilee he and all his family would go free (40-41) whether or not he had completed six years.

This was in contrast to their foreign slaves which were to be regarded as property (45). They and their descendants could be passed on to their owners' children (46) as an inheritance. The reason for this distinction was that all Israelites were God's servants. God had rescued them from slavery in Egypt to be free to serve Him (42).

Selling Themselves to a Foreigner (47-55)

If there was no relative who could afford to buy the Israelite who had become poor, he could sell himself to a wealthy foreigner living in Israel (47). His relatives were to keep an eye on things to make sure that he was treated as a hired worker and not forced to do work that was excessively strenuous (53).

He could be redeemed at any time, either by a close relative or, if his circumstances changed, by himself (48-49). The cost was to be calculated in the same way as for redeeming property, by reckoning up the number of years he had been a slave and how long before the next Jubilee (50-52). If he was not redeemed, he and his family would be set free to return to property and clan in the Jubilee (54).

Motivation

If these rules were followed they would work out for the good of Israel. The land would be cared for and so produce its best. Everybody could be sure that their descendants would not be without a means of producing food. Nobody would have to accept that they and their descendants would be slaves forever. But it is God rather than the well-being of the people who is at the heart of this chapter.

It was God who spoke to Moses on Mount Sinai and dictated these rules (1).

The land belongs to God (23). It was to be treated with respect and great care by giving it a year of rest, "a Sabbath to the LORD" (2, 4). In that phrase it is God who is in focus rather than the land. Because the land is God's, when negotiating to buy or sell property, the fear of God ensured that a fair price was paid (17).

148

All Israelites belonged to God, they were His servants (55). So the fear of God was to prevent them from wronging one another in the buying and selling of property (14, 17), and in the way they treated a fellow Israelite working for them (36, 43).

They were reminded that their God was the LORD (1, 2, 4, 17), who had rescued them from slavery in Egypt (38, 42, 55), and to whom, therefore, they owed everything.

Failure

There are references to the principles underlying the instructions of Leviticus 25 in the record of the history of Israel. Boaz redeemed the property which Naomi's husband evidently sold before they went to Moab (Ruth 3-4). Naboth referred to the vineyard which King Ahab coveted as "the inheritance of my fathers" (1Kings 21:3). King Zedekiah proclaimed freedom for slaves (Jeremiah 34:8). Nehemiah was angry when the Jews took advantage of the poverty of their fellow Jews (Nehemiah 5).

But there is no record of the Year of Jubilee being observed. In fact the prophets complained about "those who join house to house, who add field to field" (Isaiah 5:8). They pronounced judgment on those who "trample on the needy" and "buy the poor for silver" (Amos 8:4-6). They denounced those who "covet fields and seize them, and houses and take them away" (Micah 2:2). So it is evident that by the eighth century BC the instructions of Leviticus 25 were being ignored.

It may not come as a surprise that these instructions were neglected. They are not easy to obey. They require great generosity of spirit, a genuine concern for the well-being of one's fellow man, a willingness to pursue his well-being at cost to oneself, and a strong belief in a God who cares and will provide even against the odds.

Jubilee Today

Leviticus 25 is a reminder that the whole of Creation is God's, and that the fear of Him should control the way we treat the environment and others. He demands that there should be no exploitation of land or people. The chapter shows that God is on the side of the poor and has put in the hands of the rich the means of lifting them out of poverty.

God has not changed. We are still called upon to do good and lend, even to the undeserving, without expecting anything in return (Luke 6:35-36). We should do this because that is what our Heavenly Father does. Failure to live in this way results in the rich getting richer and the poor getting poorer.

It is worth noticing that God's intention was not simply to forgive debt. It was rather that, through the generous help of their brother Israelites, means and opportunity should be given to the one in poverty to get himself out of trouble. The Jubilee was a last resort.

Caring for the poor must include caring for the environment. The instructions about the Sabbatical years come first in this chapter because the health of the land is essential to the health of the people. It would have been pointless returning property to the original owners if, in their absence, the land had been rendered unfit to grow food. Today, the continuous demands of rich countries to get what they want when they want it is wrecking God's world, and it is the poor countries which are suffering the most from that. Christians need to consider carefully how their way of life is contributing to that process.

Three Questions

It may help to ask ourselves three questions.

Is our worship of God real? Hosea told the people of Israel that they did not really know God, and that was shown by their behaviour towards one another (Hosea 4:1-2). Their response was, "Let us return to the LORD" (Hosea 6:1-3). They evidently thought that returning to the LORD meant performing religious rituals, because God's reply was, "I desire steadfast love and not sacrifice, the knowledge of God rather than burnt offerings" (Hosea 6:6). Their love, God said, was like a mist which would disappear as soon as the sun came up (Hosea 6:4). The love and worship God wanted was something that would be in operation every day and in all circumstances. Isaiah preached a similar message to Judah (Isaiah 58:6). Real worship is not just what we do in church services. It involves our whole selves, our whole lives (Romans 12:1-2).

Where do we place our trust for well-being and security? Five times in the Sermon on the Mount the Lord Jesus told us not to be anxious (Matthew 6:25-34), because our Heavenly Father, who feeds the birds and clothes the flowers, will provide us with what we need. Those who do not believe that will grab what they can when they can, and hoard what they cannot use immediately. This results in others going without.

What is our hope for the future? Those who believe that this life is all there is will live to please themselves without thought for how that might affect

150

others. But those who believe that sufferings in this world are not worth comparing with the glories of the next (Romans 8:18), will be willing to go without in order to meet the needs of the less fortunate.

Jesus and Jubilee

At the beginning of Jesus' ministry, when He returned to Nazareth and went to the synagogue, he was given the scroll of Isaiah from which to read (Luke 4:16-19). He chose the passage which speaks of God's Anointed One announcing "the year of the LORD's favour" in which the poor would receive good news and captives would be set free (Isaiah 61:1-2). This is obviously referring to a year of Jubilee and Jesus said that on that day, the day of His visit to Nazareth, Isaiah's prophecy had been fulfilled in their hearing (Luke 4:21).

Jesus was saying that He had come to proclaim and begin God's Jubilee. He proved that was true by setting people free from diseases and from demons (Luke 4:40-41). He proved it by setting people free from guilt by forgiving their sins (Luke 5:20-25). He continues to set people free today (John 8:32, 36; Romans 6:7, 18).

Jesus' Jubilee will be perfectly fulfilled when those who trust Him will be set free from the very presence of sin (1 John 3:2-3), and poverty and suffering will be gone forever (Revelation 21:3-4). That Jubilee, like that of Leviticus 25, will be announced by the sound of a trumpet, the trumpet of God (1 Thessalonians 4:14-17).

Life-or-Death Decisions
Leviticus 26

From infancy we begin to learn that there are good and bad ways of doing things, right and wrong ways of behaving. This is true in the family, in education, in employment and in society at large. We learn that doing what is good and right brings rewards of one kind or another, while doing what is bad or wrong may result in punishment, pain or loss. The link between cause and effect is not always direct, immediate or obvious.

In many cases right and wrong are defined by the rules of the society in which we find ourselves. But often something is right or wrong simply because that is the way the world works. Gravity is essential to life on this planet; disregard it and a fall could result in injury or death. Fire is useful, but play with it and you could get burned. Husband and wife strengthen the union of their lives through the sexual union of their bodies, but the ultimate outcome of promiscuity is disease.

This is God's world, so it is not surprising that, having given His covenant people the rules by which He wanted them to live, He went on to encourage them by telling them of the good things that would follow obedience while warning them of the perils of disobedience.

Obedience and its Rewards

The chapter begins with commands about idolatry, God's Sabbaths and God's sanctuary and by reminding them that He is the LORD their God. This summarises the Law in a nutshell. Giving due regard to these things would require obedience to every detail of the Law.

God promised that if they would live in obedience to Him, they would never suffer hunger. He would send the autumn rain to prepare the land for sowing and to ensure the seeds would germinate and the plants would grow. He would send the spring rains to swell the ears and produce a good crop of grain (4). They would never have times of hunger, waiting for the next harvest before they could eat again (5). In fact, sometimes there would be more than enough (10).

God promised security (5). They would not work hard on their farms only for their food to be stolen by foreign raiders (6). He would ensure that wild beasts did not threaten them or their herds and flocks (6). If they were invaded by foreign armies, they would be victorious even though they were overwhelmingly outnumbered (7-8).

The result of this prosperity and security would be that the population would grow (9) and so God would fulfil the covenant first made to Abraham (Genesis 17:1-8).

Obedience would also bring spiritual blessings. God would make permanent His dwelling with them (11) and would even walk among them as in Eden (12). So God's purpose in rescuing them from Egypt would be fulfilled. They would "walk erect", free from imposed burdens, heads held high, a proud people, God's people (12-13).

The Consequences of Disobedience

The consequences of disobedience would be in stark contrast to the blessings that would result from obedience. They would follow in five phases. Each phase would be of increasing severity, as the use of the word "sevenfold" indicates (18, 21, 24, 28).

At first they would suffer ill health. This would affect their mental state so that they would lose their confidence, panic and run from imaginary foes, and leave their harvests for their enemies to eat (14-17).

Then God would withhold the rains so that they would be unable to cultivate their land, and there would be no fruit on their trees. Any pride they had in their own abilities to provide for themselves would be broken. They would be reminded that they depended upon God for their existence (18-20).

In the third phase God would let loose the wild beasts which He had kept in check. Children and livestock would fall prey to these animals and the population would be depleted (21-22).

If by this time the people had not returned to God, He would become their enemy. They would be under constant attack from foreign armies, and they should know from this that all these disasters were happening because they had broken the covenant. They would run for shelter to their cities but would there suffer disease and famine, the usual results of siege. Famine would be so severe that, instead of every household having its own oven, one oven would suffice for ten families. Bread would be rationed and no-one would get enough (23-26).

Finally the shortage of food would become so severe that they would resort to cannibalism (29). They would eat the children who were their hope for the

153

future, who were to have been the fulfilment of God's covenant promise. War would leave dead bodies lying around, many on the very altars of the false gods to which they had turned (30). The land and the cities would be totally destroyed and it would do no good appealing to God for help by offering sacrifices (31-33). Those who remained alive would be taken into exile. In exile they would live in weakness and fear, and many would die there (36-39).

God's Purpose

The people were warned (14, 18, 21, 23, 27) that if they did not respond by turning back to God, worse would follow. The warnings and the gradual increase in the severity of the consequences show that God's purpose was, through discipline, to bring His people back to Himself.

Although God would use foreign nations such as Assyria and Babylon to achieve these things, He makes it clear that He Himself is doing this (24, 28, 32). God would be personally dealing out the punishment for their sins and the sins of their ancestors (39). This should have been a warning to them that there was no escape. It would do no good to call on other powers to help them against their oppressors as they did in Hosea's day (Hosea 7:11). But it should also have been a comfort. The one who was dealing with them was the LORD their God who had rescued them from Egypt and wanted the very best for them. David chose to be dealt with by God rather than by men (2 Samuel 24:14) because of God's great mercy.

Hope for the Future

God's word about the land does not end with total desolation and waste. He says that while they were in exile the land would enjoy the Sabbaths which the people should have allowed while in occupation (34-35). The purpose of those Sabbaths was that the land would recover naturally and not become a dust-bowl. This indicates that God had in mind that His people would come back to the land and that it would be ready for their return. This is the connection in thought between verses 42 and 43 in which God says that He will remember His covenants with Jacob, Isaac and Abraham, he will remember the land and the land will enjoy its Sabbaths. He goes on to promise that he would never completely destroy His people or forget His covenant with them, because He is the LORD their God (44-45).

This restoration of the people to the land would be dependent upon their change of heart. They would have to recognise that the heart of the nation was uncircumcised (41). However conscientiously they had performed the rite of physical circumcision, their hearts were sinful and, by their behaviour, they had broken the covenant. They would have to confess their sins (40), and make amends (41) by suffering in exile and turning back to God. Then God would remember His covenant and restore the people to the land and to fellowship with Him.

Past Fulfilment

There were times in the history of Israel when the nation briefly experienced the blessings of obedience. For instance, during Solomon's reign the people were as numerous as sand on the seashore. They had plenty to eat and drink and were happy. Solomon reigned over all the neighbouring countries so that the people lived in peace and safety (1 Kings 4:20-25).

But it seems that periods of disobedience were more numerous and longer than episodes of obedience.

The book of Judges gives a clear picture of a recurring cycle of disobedience by the people, punishment at the hands of enemies, and rescue by a God-appointed judge. The restoration of the people to the obedient worship of God was transitory, and the cycle began again with their disobedience. During the time of Gideon, Israel did what was evil in God's eyes, and God allowed the Midianites to oppress them for seven years. The Midianites would invade the land, steal the crops and livestock, and "they laid waste the land" (Judges 6:1-5). There were wild beasts in the land in those days (Judges 14:5).

The same picture is repeated during the years of the monarchy; some kings honoured God, but many were idolaters and led the nation in evil ways. Even King Solomon in later life turned away from the LORD to worship the false gods of his many wives (1 Kings 11:1-6). The consequences of disobedience followed as God raised up adversaries against Solomon (1 Kings 11:14, 23).

God's warning of exile was fulfilled for the northern kingdom of Israel in 722BC, when Assyria deported the people and scattered them throughout the Assyrian empire. The fulfilment for the southern kingdom of Judah began in 605BC when a number of Jews, Daniel among them, were taken into exile in Babylon. In 597BC another group including Ezekiel were exiled. In 587BC Jerusalem and the Temple were destroyed by the Babylonians and the last group of Jews to be exiled were taken away. All this happened because God's people turned away from Him.

Jesus pronounced woes on the religious leaders of His day. He said they were hypocrites, all outward show, but inwardly full of greed, self-indulgence and lawlessness (Matthew 23:25-28). Looking over Jerusalem He said that its house had been left desolate (Matthew 23:38). He meant that God had departed from the Temple (cf. Ezekiel 10 & 11), and He told His disciples that the Temple would be destroyed (Matthew 14:2). This was fulfilled in AD70.

So God's promise of blessings for obedience and warnings of oppression, destruction and exile as the consequences of disobedience were fulfilled throughout Israel's history. At the same time, Jews have retained their national identity in spite of being dispersed throughout the world for centuries. For decades now they have been returning to Palestine and establishing a state of Israel. God has been keeping His promise to remember His covenant while they are in exile and not destroy them completely (44-45).

Present Application

God's involvement in the affairs of the world is not confined to one nation. God is showing His wrath against all unrighteousness and ungodliness by meting out the due penalty for error, regardless of race (Romans 1:18-27).

In the context of Romans 1, it is evident that God's wrath is active through the normal course of events; this is the way God has made His world to work. God's wrath is at work in an impersonal way. But God does deal personally with individuals, as the experience of Job shows, and directly with nations, as the prophets make clear. With which people is God dealing personally and directly in these days?

Israel is still God's covenant people (Romans 11:29), but "not all who are descended from Israel belong to Israel" (Romans 9:6). People of other nations will listen to Christ and come to Him and He will be the shepherd of one flock (John 10:16). The apostles would be the spiritual leaders of this new Israel (Matthew 19:28), in which there is no distinction between Jew and Gentile, but all are beneficiaries of God's promises (Galatians 3:28-29).

God deals directly with His Church. It is a dwelling place for God by His Spirit (Ephesians 2:22). Christ stands in the midst of the churches and sends a message to each church that is relevant to the local needs (Revelation 1-3). So the promise of Leviticus 26:11-12 is being fulfilled.

156

There were times in the early years of the Church when God did deal directly in judgment because of sin. Ananias and Sapphira lied to the Holy Spirit by pretending to be more generous in their giving than they really were. They died as a direct result of that (Acts 5:1-11). Some members of the church in Corinth suffered illness and some died because they were abusing the Lord's Supper (1 Corinthians 11:17-30). Both these cases may be understood as God disciplining His people as a father would his children (Hebrews 12:4-12). The Church had to learn from the start that God cannot be deceived and that His sacred things must be treated with awe and respect.

The book of Job shows that suffering is not always the result of sin. Conversely, just because people are enjoying God's gifts of sun and rain it does not mean that they are living obedient, godly lives (Matthew 5:45). Paul, who served his Lord as faithfully as anyone could, had a very mixed experience of God's provision. He learned to deal with "plenty and hunger, abundance and need" (Philippians 4:12). Jesus did not promise His disciples an easy life. He said that anyone who wished to follow Him would have to deny themselves and take up the cross (Mark 8:34). But He promised that those who suffered for His sake would receive a great reward in heaven (Matthew 5:11-12).

Most importantly, the blessings experienced through Christ are spiritual; God "has blessed us in Christ with every spiritual blessing in the heavenly places" (Ephesians 1:3). For example, Paul experienced God's blessing in that Christ strengthened him to deal with any and every situation (Philippians 4:13). We can never lose these blessings because Christ has borne the curse for us (Galatians 3:10-14), that is, He has borne all the consequences of our disobedience. The covenant which promises the blessings and freedom from all fear of punishment, has been sealed with the blood of Christ (Matthew 26:27-28). God will never forget that covenant.

Future Fulfilment

When Jesus comes into His own, the promises of the blessings of obedience will be perfectly fulfilled. God will dwell among His people (Ezekiel 37:24-27). The population will grow (Ezekiel 36:10-12). There will be places to live and food to eat because ruins will be rebuilt and the land will be so productive that farmers will struggle to bring in the harvest before the time for sowing comes round again (Amos 9:13-15). God's people will be safe from

157

their enemies and will live without fear (Ezekiel 34:28). Wolves will live with lambs, leopards will lie down with goats and wild animals will follow little children around (Isaiah 11:6-9). All this will come about in a new heaven and a new earth which God will create (Revelation 21:1, 5).

On that day we will all stand before Christ's judgment seat (2 Corinthians 5:10) so that we may receive what is due to us according to the way we have spent our lives. If our names are written in the Lamb's book of life, we have no reason to fear the lake of fire (Revelation 20:15). But our service for Him will be tested by fire and we may gain a reward or suffer loss according to what passes that test (1 Corinthians 3:10-25).

There will be a crown of life for those who remain faithful through trials (James 1:12). There will be a crown of glory for church leaders who have served their flocks unselfishly and with genuine care, while setting a good example (1 Peter 5:4). Paul was able to say that he had fought the good fight, he had finished the race and he had kept the faith. A crown was ready and waiting for him as a reward for his God-pleasing life (2 Timothy 4:7-8).

In that place of glory in which there is only total obedience, God will dwell with mankind. They will be His people and God himself will be with them as their God (Revelation 21:3). So the promise of Leviticus 26:11-12 will be completely and perfectly fulfilled.

A Grateful Response
Leviticus 27

A Rash Vow

At a time when the Ammonites were attacking Israel, the elders of Gilead called Jephthah back from exile to lead them in battle (Judges 11). Jephthah tried diplomacy but the king of Ammon would not listen so Jephthah went on the attack. Before he went he made a vow to the LORD that, if He would give the victory to Jephthah, he would offer as a burnt offering whatever first came out of his house to greet him on his return. Jephthah defeated the Ammonites and returned home. As he approached his house, his only child, his daughter came out to meet him. It seems that Jephthah kept his vow and his daughter was killed and her body burnt.

What a rash vow! He must have known that no animal would come out of his house. He may have thought that it would be a slave. Even so, if he had known God better he would have known that human sacrifice was unacceptable to Him. If he had known God better he would have known that the way to victory over Israel's enemies was for the nation and its leaders to live in obedience to the LORD (Leviticus 26). But he lived in days when everyone did what was right in their own eyes (Judges 21:25). Jephthah and his daughter suffered terribly for that.

God's Provision

Making a vow was not required, it was voluntary, and it was no sin not to make a vow (Deuteronomy 23:21-23). But once a vow was made to the LORD it was binding, and failing to fulfil it was sin. The sin offering was available to deal with that (5:1-13).

However careful a person was, a vow might be made which the one who had made the vow found that he could or would rather not fulfil. In the final chapter of Leviticus God made gracious provision for paying a prescribed sum of money to redeem the pledge. At the same time the rules given tended to discourage the making of vows without careful thought. Redemption could be costly.

Dedicating Persons

A vow might be made which involved dedicating a person to the LORD (2-8). The one making the vow might dedicate themselves or, as in the case of Hannah (1 Samuel 1:11), someone else. This would have meant the subject of the vow spending their life working in the sanctuary. But the work there was the privilege of the priests and Levites and, with the addition of people who were the subject of vows, the sanctuary would soon have become overcrowded. So the solution was for the one who had made the vow to pay a sum of money by way of redemption.

The economy of Israel was based on manual labour. So the prices for redemption were set according to the ability of the person to carry out productive work. The price was to be paid in silver shekels, and the weight of silver in a shekel was defined by the priests (25). The young and the old could not be as productive as those in their prime. In general, men would be more productive than women. So prices were set as follows: for an infant aged between one month and five years, the price would be five shekels for a boy and three shekels for a girl (6); for those aged between five and twenty years, the price would be twenty shekels for a male and ten shekels for a female (5); for those aged between twenty and sixty years, the price would be fifty shekels for a man (3) and thirty shekels for a woman (4); for those over sixty years the price would be fifteen shekels for a man and ten shekels for a woman (7). The fact that women in their prime were valued more highly than a male at any other age shows that they were an essential asset in that society.

God made provision for a case where someone had made a vow which he could not afford to redeem (8). Then the priest was to set a value on the dedicated person according to what the one who made the vow could afford.

It is thought that the wage for a month was one shekel. So the minimum cost of redeeming a vow involving a person would be three months' wages (6). The cost of redeeming a man in his prime would be the wages of more than four years (3). These rules should have made people think very carefully before dedicating themselves or someone else to the LORD.

Firstborn sons could not be subjects of a vow. They belonged to God already because He had saved the firstborn Hebrew sons when the firstborn of Egypt had been killed (Exodus 13:13-15). Firstborn sons in Israel had to be redeemed when they were one month old by the payment of five shekels (Numbers 18:15-16).

Dedicating Animals

Animals could be dedicated to the LORD (9-13). The procedures for dealing with an animal given to God as a vow offering are set out in 3:1-17 and

160

7:11-18. When such a vow was made there was no going back, the whole animal was holy (9), it became God's property. The worshipper could not decide that the animal he had given was too good and try to exchange it for another. If he tried to do so then he would have to give up both animals (10). This would have encouraged people to think carefully before they made a vow.

Unclean animals, those not acceptable for sacrifice, could also be subjects of vows (11). The priest could either make use of such an animal or sell it. If the worshipper wished to redeem it he would have to pay what the priest decided was its value plus one fifth (12-13).

Dedicating Property

In view of the laws about Jubilee (25:25-34), the houses referred to in verses 14 and 15 must be houses in walled cities. Such houses were not part of a family's inheritance from God so could be bought and sold. They could be put to use in God's service by the priests using or selling them. If the one who had made the vow wished to redeem his property he had to pay the priest's valuation plus one fifth (15).

Property not within a walled city, a house with its fields, could be dedicated to God even though it was the family's inheritance. The priests would benefit from what the land produced through the owner working it. The value was calculated according to "its seed" (16). This could mean either the value of the seed required to sow it or the value of the expected harvest. The other factor in determining its value was the number of years from the time when the owner wished to redeem it until the next Jubilee (17-18). The price of redemption would be the value plus one fifth (19).

A man might dedicate a field then sell it to avoid having to work the land for the priests. If this was done, or the option of redemption was not taken up, then when Jubilee came the land would become the property of the priests (20-21) and it could not be redeemed. This eliminated the possibility of someone dedicating property to God, selling it then receiving it back for nothing in Jubilee.

If a field that was not part of the family's inheritance but had been bought from another family was vowed (22), for it to be redeemed the valuation plus one fifth had to be paid immediately (23). In the year of Jubilee it would be returned to its original owner (24).

161

Limitations

The firstborn of any animal that could be offered in sacrifice already belonged to God (Numbers 18:17), so could not be vowed (26). The firstborn of an unclean animal could be vowed but it had to be either redeemed at the valuation plus one fifth, or be sold at the valuation (27).

Nothing and nobody that God had said must be destroyed could be redeemed (28-29). This could be someone who sacrificed to another god (Exodus 22:20), or property seized in battle (Joshua 7:1-22).

The first mention of the giving of one tenth is on the occasion when Abram met Melchizedek (Genesis 14:18-20), who is described as "priest of God Most High". Jacob vowed to give God a tenth of all that God gave him (Genesis 28:13-22). The giving of tithes to the Levites for their support is written into the Law in Numbers 18:21-29 and Deuteronomy 14:22-29. Since the tithe was required by God it could not be the subject of a vow (30). The tithe would be from the fields and trees or from the flocks and herds. It could be redeemed by paying its value plus one fifth (31). Animals were selected for the tithe by separating out every tenth animal to "pass under the herdsman's staff" (32). This was to eliminate the possibility of the owner choosing the worst animals for the tithe and keeping the best for himself (33). In a sense, the animals made the choice by the way they lined up to pass the herdsman. If the owner tried to substitute a worse animal for a better, he would forfeit both (33).

Bargaining or Giving Thanks

Some Old Testament characters made a vow to give something to God if He would first do something for them. Thus Hannah promised that if God would answer her prayer for a son she would give him back to God (1 Samuel 1:11). Absalom told David his father that he had vowed that if the LORD would bring him back to Jerusalem he would worship Him (2 Samuel 15:7-8). It is not clear whether or not he really had made that vow, and it could be argued that worship was God's due anyway.

But some made their vow in response to what God had promised to do or had already done. God promised Jacob that He would fulfil all the promises He had made to Abraham in Jacob, and that He would never leave him until all that was done. In response, Jacob vowed to give God tithes of everything (Genesis 28:13-22). David said that he must perform his vows to God because God had delivered his soul from death (Psalm 56:12-13). Jonah's declaration that what he had vowed he would pay (Jonah 2:9) was in response to the certainty that God had heard his prayer (Jonah 2:2, 7) and was saving him (Jonah 2:4, 6). If a Christian were to make a vow, gratitude for what God has done would be the more fitting motive.

Good Advice

The advice given by the Preacher (Ecclesiastes 5:1-7) is to think carefully before making a vow. Vows may be made in times of stress as in Jephthah's case, accompanying a prayer that God will meet a need. They may also be made in response to God's answer to such a prayer. In either case, the stress or the sense of wonder and gratitude can be so great that they result in a vow being made which is unreasonable. So, think before you make a vow.

The Preacher also advises that if a vow is made it should be paid as soon as possible, and that it is better not to vow at all than to vow and not pay. What makes the making of a vow especially serious is that, as the story of Jephthah seems to show, God, on His part, honours the vow, however unwise that vow is.

Vows in the New Testament

There are two records in the New Testament of Christians putting themselves under a vow (Acts 18:18; 21:23). In both cases it was Jewish Christians that were involved and in both instances it was done so that Paul could be "all things to all people" (1 Corinthians 9:19-23). Jesus said that the making of vows was a Jewish tradition and that making the keeping of a vow more important than the keeping of God's law is hypocrisy, play-acting and empty worship (Matthew 15:3-9).

Principles of Giving

Making and fulfilling a vow is essentially giving something to God which is over and above what God has demanded. During the time Paul was teaching the new Christians in Antioch, there was a famine. So the Christians in Antioch determined that they would send relief to their fellow-believers in Judea (Acts 11:29). The word translated "determined" conveys the idea of setting a fence around something. The money they determined to send was set aside for God and was not to be used for anything else. In effect, they made a vow without it becoming entangled in Jewish tradition. This practice is encouraged in the New Testament.

The motivation to give comes from two sources. One is the needs of others (Acts 11:29; 2 Corinthians 8:13). The other is the generous grace of the Lord Jesus in giving up His riches for our sake (2 Corinthians 8:9). In view of that, Christians should be generous and willing in their giving (2 Corinthians 9:6-7). In generosity we should avoid ostentation. We do not give to impress our fellow believers but to please God. Anything else can result in pretence and lies, as in the case of Ananias and Sapphira (Acts 5:1-11), who made a show of generosity.

We should avoid making rash vows to give more than we can afford. We are to give according to our ability (Acts 11:29; 1 Corinthians 16:2; 2 Corinthians 8:12). The purpose of giving is not to put ourselves in need but to meet the needs of others, to make things more equal (2 Corinthians 8:13-14). We are most likely to achieve these things if we regularly and systematically set aside what we are able to give (1 Corinthians 16:2), rather than responding to an appeal without careful thought.

Giving one tenth is a good starting point, but the tithe is not commanded anywhere in the New Testament. In fact, Jesus said that meticulously tithing everything was a lightweight matter compared with being just, merciful and faithful (Matthew 23:23). As already noted, our giving should be determined, not by calculating one tenth, but by the need and by our ability to give, while bearing in mind the Lord's amazing generosity. The widow's penny (Mark 12:41-44) was of more value in Jesus' eyes than the huge gifts of the rich. They gave what they could easily afford, she gave all she had.

The most important aspect of the giving of the Christians of Macedonia was that "they gave themselves first to the Lord" (2 Corinthians 8:5). This should be at the heart of our giving. We are not our own, we have been bought at the cost of the life of the Lord Jesus (1 Corinthians 6:19-20). So our aim should be to glorify God in all that we do, including in our giving.

A Fitting Conclusion

Leviticus begins with God, having made His dwelling place with His people, setting out the means by which that relationship could be maintained. It would involve sacrifice. It would mean living lives that were God-pleasing. It would not be easy, especially as their way of life would be in stark contrast to those of the nations around them. But it would be worth it. An unbroken relationship with the LORD would guarantee their safety, health and prosperity. So the last chapter, in which is envisaged a grateful response to their God and all that He had done and had promised, is a fitting end to the book.

#0059 - 021117 - C0 - 210/148/9 - PB - DID2012903